Y.O.U.
YEARNING OF
Understanding

Unveiling the Truths That
Lie Beneath the Surface

ALEXIS N. MOORE

WWW.SELFPUBLISHN30DAYS.COM

Published by *Self Publish -N- 30 Days*

© Copyright 2024   Alexis N. Moore

All rights reserved worldwide. No part of this book may be reproduced or transmitted in any form or by any means, electronic or mechanical, including photocopying, recording, or by any information storage and retrieval system without written permission from Alexis N. Moore.

Printed in the United States of America

ISBN: 979-8-87226-915-1
1. Self-Help 2. Inspirational 3. Growth
Alexis N. Moore, *Y.O.U.*

Disclaimer/Warning:

This book is intended for lecture and informative purposes only. This publication is designed to provide competent and reliable information regarding the subject matter covered. The author or publisher is not engaged in rendering legal or professional advice. Laws vary from state to state, and if legal, financial, or other expert assistance is needed, the services of a professional should be sought. The author and publisher disclaim any liability that is incurred from the use or application of the contents of this book.

TABLE OF CONTENTS

	Introduction	1
①	The Root of Who You Are	7
②	Hidden Pain	23
③	Facing Your Fears	37
④	Cultivating Courage and Strength	55
⑤	Breaking Free from Doubt	67
⑥	It's Okay to Pause	85
⑦	Open Mouths, Open Doors	93
⑧	Unveiling the Desires of Your Heart	105
	Conclusion	123

Introduction

Trees can't survive and thrive without nurturing and anchoring roots. But let us not be deceived. Some individuals may appear as mighty trees on the surface, exuding accomplishment and success. However, if we dare to look below the surface, we may unearth roots that are feeble or practically nonexistent. What happens when someone lacks strong roots or has compromised ones? It is akin to a tree deprived of the nourishment vital for its survival.

Without healthy roots, we find ourselves famished for love, which inevitably affects every aspect of our lives. Why is this so? Simply put, everything requires a root. To truly feel secure in life, we must be loved and nurtured. We must recognize our origins and embrace the unbreakable bond with our ancestors.

Our roots become the wellspring of our emotional and spiritual sustenance. Just as a tree requires sturdy roots and a robust trunk to bear fruit, our own roots provide the foundation for our growth. If the roots begin to deteriorate, the entire tree suffers a similar fate.

The intriguing aspect of roots lies in their duality. While they remain hidden beneath the surface, roots serve as the very catalyst for a tree's growth. Majestic trees flourish and expand outward with uninhibited freedom, always cognizant of their deep-seated roots, their grounding force. It has been said that a tree is the only entity capable of simultaneous growth in two directions: Its roots grow downward as its branches reach skyward. Consider this: A bird must first have a protective nest before it can soar through the skies. When we possess a nurturing nest to return to, we gain the confidence to fly securely. Our confidence stems from the nurturing we receive within our sanctuary.

> *Our confidence stems from the nurturing we receive within our sanctuary.*

On the surface, those who lack a nest may appear to be flying, perhaps even achieving great heights. Yet, their flight is not fortified by security. True security grants us the freedom to explore. The most audacious explorers are those unencumbered by fear, and fearlessness arises from a place of security.

Integrity, much like the trunk of a tree, embodies solidity. While roots remain predominantly hidden underground, providing an indispensable foundation for upward and outward growth, a tree also exhibits a visible, strong trunk above ground. Trees are renowned

Introduction

for their resolute strength. It withstands the fiercest storms, bending gracefully yet refusing to be toppled.

The trunk symbolizes values. What do you truly believe in? What is your purpose in life? This is where I found myself not too long ago, which led me to write this book.

Nothing could shake the profound peace and graceful flow that I exhibited...until life took an unexpected turn, snatching away my six-figure job and blessing me with the surprise of pregnancy, giving birth to my beautiful daughter, Aliyah Moore.

It hasn't been easy to leave behind everyone and everything I know, but I am determined to embark on a journey of self-discovery.

I was once an exceptional student-athlete, blessed with a full basketball scholarship to TSU and earning my BBA in Accounting within a remarkable four years. Fresh out of college, I ventured into the oil and gas industry, where success seemed to be an unending ascent. However, as fate would have it, the pendulum swung the other way, leaving me without a job, relying on food stamps, and with no clear direction except for my unwavering faith.

Through the power of self-discipline, mental toughness, and resilience, I underwent a remarkable transformation. I shed the weight of depression and emerged as a co-owner of a Smoothie King Franchise alongside my sister, Sade Moore. We embarked on this entrepreneurial journey, defying the odds and creating a thriving business.

Y.O.U.

But my journey didn't stop there. I also stepped into the realm of Muscle Mania Fitness Competitions, defying expectations and showcasing my inner strength.

> *Within the depths of my soul, there has always been a yearning for understanding.*

Through these pages, I invite you to join me on a journey of inspiration and discovery. My purpose in writing this book is simple yet profound: to ignite a flicker of hope within your heart and remind you that no matter how insurmountable challenges may seem, you can make it too. Life's trials and tribulations may have left you battered and bruised, but I stand here as living proof that the darkest moments can become catalysts for the most radiant transformations.

Within the depths of my soul, there has always been a yearning for understanding. It's as if I could sense the truths that lay just beneath the surface, waiting to be unveiled. This book is the manifestation of that yearning—a heartfelt endeavor to share my own journey, peel back the layers of vulnerability, and expose the profound lessons that have shaped me into the woman I am today.

I will take you by the hand and guide you through the corridors of my life, revealing the moments of despair, the pivotal choices, and the divine encounters that have sculpted the very essence of my being. It is not a journey for the faint of heart, but it promises to unearth the hidden treasures buried within crevices of pain.

Introduction

This is not just a book; it is an invitation to embark on a quest for truth and discovering who we are. Together, we will unravel the tangled threads of our past, confront the shadows that have haunted us for far too long, and boldly step into the light of our redemption. It is time to shed the shackles of doubt, and reclaim our rightful place as warriors of resilience.

May my story challenge your beliefs, provoke your emotions, and ignite your spirit. We will confront the questions that have lingered in the depths of our souls, and we will find solace in the realization that our struggles are not in vain—that they have a purpose far greater than we could ever comprehend.

The truths that await us are not always easy to face, but they possess a transformative power that will reshape the very fabric of our existence. It is in the exploration of these truths that we will find healing, restoration, and a renewed sense of purpose. It is through the vulnerability of sharing our stories that we will connect with others on a profound level, inspiring them to embrace their own journeys of triumph.

Together, let us embark on a journey of self-discovery, where hope shines through the cracks of brokenness and where dreams take flight amidst the ashes of disappointment. By the time you reach the final page, I hope you will emerge with a renewed sense of purpose, armed with the unwavering belief that you, too, can make it.

Chapter 1
The Root of Who You Are

"The more rooted you are in yourself, the more powerful you are, and the more you are able to create the life you want."
—Bryant McGill

When we think of a tree, our minds often conjure up images of a large trunk with branches and leaves spreading outwards, creating a beautiful canopy. These branches and leaves are like our external appearance, and much like a tree, we tend to focus on what is visible on the surface, forgetting what lies beneath. If I asked you to draw a picture of a tree, you might include intricate details, such as the texture of the bark or the intricate patterns on the leaves.

As a child, I used to add a bird's nest on the branches and a hole in the center of the trunk where I imagined a family of squirrels lived. Yet, rarely do we include the roots of the tree in our artistic representations.

The roots of a tree are like the foundation of our being, often overlooked and ignored. Just as a tree cannot survive without strong roots, we cannot thrive without a solid foundation. Let us explore the importance of nurturing our roots so that we can grow to our full potential, just like a tree with deep roots can reach for the sky. Bryant McGill's quote at the beginning of this chapter speaks to the importance of being grounded in oneself and one's own identity.

> *When we are truly rooted in ourselves, we have a deep understanding of who we are, what we stand for, and what we want out of life.*

When we are truly rooted in ourselves, we have a deep understanding of who we are, what we stand for, and what we want out of life. This inner strength and clarity allow us to pursue our goals and dreams with confidence and conviction.

On the other hand, when we lack a strong sense of self or are not rooted in our values and beliefs, we may feel lost or uncertain about our path in life. We may be easily swayed by the opinions and expectations of others, or we may struggle to make decisions that align with our true desires and purposes.

By taking the time to cultivate a strong sense of self-awareness and personal growth, we can strengthen our roots and become more

The Root of Who You Are

powerful individuals. This may involve exploring our values and beliefs, reflecting on our past experiences, and learning to trust our intuition and inner wisdom.

Ultimately, the more rooted we are in ourselves, the more we can create the life we want. We have the power to shape our reality and pursue our dreams with purpose and passion.

Uncover Your Flaws

We often focus on the things that others can see, such as our weight, our makeup, or our clothing. We try to hide our perceived flaws and accentuate what we believe to be our best features. As a woman, I understand this all too well. I spent years fixating on the external and never taking the time to see my inner strength.

> *To truly address our personal issues and grow as individuals, we need to be willing to take off the mask and get vulnerable with ourselves.*

Just like makeup can be used as a temporary fix to cover up blemishes and flaws, we may sometimes use distractions or temporary fixes to avoid dealing with our personal issues. We may try to bury our feelings or put on a facade to appear as though everything is okay, but just like makeup, this is only a temporary solution.

To truly address our personal issues and grow, we need to be willing to take off the mask and get vulnerable with ourselves. This means confronting the things that make us uncomfortable, whether it be past trauma, unhealthy habits, or negative self-talk.

Much like how a good skincare routine involves cleansing and caring for the skin, taking care of ourselves involves developing healthy habits and coping mechanisms. This can include regular exercise, therapy, journaling, and mindfulness practices.

It is important to remember that personal growth is a journey, and there will be ups and downs along the way. Just as a blemish may reappear after being covered up with makeup, personal issues may resurface even after we have addressed them. However, by continuing to care for ourselves and facing our issues head-on, we can develop a stronger sense of self and live a more fulfilling life.

For me, the flaw that always seemed to get in the way was my stutter. I've stuttered for as long as I can remember, and it has followed me everywhere I go. Whether I was answering a question in class, talking to friends and family, giving directions, or even asking for the salt in a restaurant, my words would be interrupted with awkward pauses. My stutter welcomed itself like an uninvited guest, digging its heels into the ground as I tried to escape.

To hide my stutter, I would often stay quiet in group settings or avoid speaking altogether. When I did speak, I would try to cover it up with filler words or by speaking quickly, hoping that no one would notice. I would spend hours practicing what I wanted to say, trying to make sure that every word was perfect and flawless.

The Root of Who You Are

But the more I focused on hiding my stutter, the more it consumed me. It became all I could think about, and I began to define myself by my stutter. It wasn't until I started to focus on my inner strength and the things that made me unique that I began to see my stutter as just a small part of who I am.

There was no hiding from my stutter. I couldn't escape the genetic disorder that had been passed down to me from my father, and an uncle on my mother's side.

As a child, I didn't see it as an issue, and I was never treated differently. I can see them now calling me by my childhood nickname, saying, "Coco, Slow down. I don't understand you. You are talking too fast. You are trying too hard."

Family members would comment about my speech impediment. "Your dad really marked you," they would say, and I knew exactly what they meant. Not only did I physically resemble my father, but I also spoke like him, with the same stutter and hesitations. It was a constant reminder of what he had passed down to me—and there was no way I could hide it. No matter *how* hard I tried.

Accept Yourself

Do you ever feel like there's something in your life that you want to escape? Maybe there's a part of yourself that you haven't fully accepted, and it feels like a burden that you carry. It's not uncommon to feel this way, and it can be difficult to shake.

Y.O.U.

But the truth is, you are fearfully and wonderfully made. Psalm 139:14 reminds us that we are all unique and valuable and that God's works are wonderful. However, I understand that it can be challenging to accept this truth when you're struggling with something that makes you feel less than wonderful.

As someone who has struggled with a stutter for many years, I know what it's like to beg God to take away what feels like a weakness. My stutter became my "limp," just like Jacob's, and it felt like a heavy burden that I carried with me. But over time, I learned to see it as a part of who I am and to embrace it as a unique aspect of myself.

> *As someone who has struggled with a stutter for many years, I know what it's like to beg God to take away what feels like a weakness.*

The story of Jacob wrestling with God can be found in Genesis 32:22-32. In this story, Jacob wrestles with an unknown man throughout the night and eventually realizes that he has been wrestling with God himself. Despite being injured during the struggle, Jacob refuses to let go until he receives a blessing from God.

This story reminds us of the struggles that we face in our own lives, including those that we may feel like we are wrestling with God about. My struggle was my stutter, but other examples could include financial struggles, relationship issues, health problems, or personal insecurities.

The Root of Who You Are

It's not always easy to accept our flaws and imperfections, but doing so can lead to a greater sense of self-love and appreciation. Instead of seeing our struggles as weaknesses, we can view them as opportunities for transformation. So if there's something in your life that you want to escape, or a part of yourself that you haven't fully accepted, I encourage you to begin digging toward the root of the issue instead of focusing on the external things.

Remember that you are fearfully and wonderfully made and that your struggles do not define you. Embrace your unique qualities and trust that God has a plan for your life, imperfections and all.

Face and Embrace Your Flaws

Faint childhood memories of going to speech therapy in elementary school flash before me. I remember Mrs. Jackson, my speech therapist, who was the best teacher. However, I can't recall the exact moment when I was diagnosed with a speech impediment. Despite spending a lot of time in class practicing how to pronounce my THs and SHs correctly, I never felt like my speech impediment was something that held me back.

> *It was a deeply distressing realization that, despite all my efforts, the words wouldn't come out of my mouth.*

As I grew older and assumed more roles where I had to communicate, stuttering became much more than just stumbling over a few syllables in a sentence. It was a deeply distressing realization that, despite all my efforts, the words wouldn't come out of my mouth. It was as if the words were stuck in my throat, and I was powerless to release them. I would stand there, my eyes wide with panic, searching desperately for synonyms or alternative phrases that could convey the same message without me having to struggle with my speech.

The experience was frustrating and disheartening. It felt as though my brain and my mouth were disconnected, with my thoughts racing ahead while my speech lagged behind, struggling to catch up. I would often end up modifying my sentence, swapping out words and phrases in an attempt to get my point across. The result was often a distorted, mangled version of the eloquent, coherent thought that had been brewing in my head.

The word eventually came, but it was like a battle won with scars to show for it. The effort and concentration required to push through the distorted word left me drained and exhausted. Nobody else knew about the internal struggle, the silent repetition of the correct word, and the fear of being judged or misunderstood. It was distorted.

The physical and emotional anxiety is all-consuming. The shortness of breath makes it feel like you're suffocating, while the sweat on your palms is a constant reminder of the nervousness that courses through your body. The occasional light-headedness is disorienting, leaving you feeling unsteady and unsure.

The Root of Who You Are

The weight was crushing. It was a feeling of hopelessness that grew until I felt like there was nothing I could do to escape. But there were moments of respite, like when I played basketball. On the court, I didn't have to worry about the jumbled mess of words in my head. I could focus on running, jumping, and competing without the fear of stumbling over my words, but as soon as basketball ended, I started discovering who I was and who I wanted to become. Of course, this didn't come without its own set of hiccups.

You Aren't Alone

Whatever the struggle may be, it can be helpful to remember that we are not alone in our wrestling. Though Jacob wrestled with God, he was able to receive a blessing and a new name that signified his transformation.

Likewise, when we bring our struggles to God, we can experience freedom through surrender. There may be times when it feels like we are in a constant state of wrestling. But by trusting in God's plan for our lives and remaining steadfast in our faith, we can emerge from our struggles stronger and more resilient than ever before.

To truly overcome our struggles, we must get to the root of the issue and understand who we are. In the same way that a tree with weak roots cannot withstand a storm, we must strengthen our roots to weather the challenges of life.

As we wrestle with God about our struggles, we may discover

that the root of the issue goes deeper than we initially thought. It may be rooted in our past experiences, our upbringing, or our self-perceptions. By addressing these underlying issues and seeking guidance from God, we will stay grounded and grow into the image that he has called us to.

Just like a tree that is pruned and cared for, we must also take care of ourselves and nurture our spiritual growth. This can involve reading scripture, praying, meditating, and seeking support from a community of faith. By doing so, we can deepen our understanding of ourselves and God, and become better equipped to have a great quality of life. In the end, the story of Jacob wrestling with God reminds us that struggle and transformation are intertwined.

> *As we wrestle with God about our struggles, we may discover that the root of the issue goes deeper than we initially thought.*

I was keenly aware of the damage to my self-confidence and self-esteem. The fear of being judged, ridiculed, or misunderstood was a constant presence, always lurking in the background. Yet despite all of this, I persevered, determined to find ways to express myself despite my challenges with stuttering. It was difficult, but one that ultimately taught me to value the power of communication, and how to embrace the struggles of life because in the end, it will be one of your biggest testimonies.

The Root of Who You Are

Beneath the Surface

The root of who you are is a complex and multifaceted concept that can be approached from different perspectives. From a psychological standpoint, your personality traits, values, beliefs, and behaviors are influenced by a combination of genetic, environmental, and cultural factors that have shaped your identity over time. Your personal experiences, relationships, and social interactions also play a significant role in shaping who you are.

Getting to know who you are and understanding the root of your identity can be a complex and ongoing process that may involve self-reflection, introspection, and exploration. Here are some suggestions that might help:

Reflect on your values and beliefs

Think about what is important to you, what you believe in, and what you stand for. Your values and beliefs are a key part of your identity. You might reflect on your values and beliefs by asking yourself questions like:

- What are my core values? (e.g., honesty, kindness, loyalty)
- What beliefs do I hold about the world and my place in it? (e.g., the importance of environmental sustainability, and the value of education)
- What issues do I feel strongly about? (e.g., social justice, animal rights, mental health awareness)

- How do my values and beliefs influence my decisions and actions?
- What are some of my flaws?
- What personality traits do I love about myself?

By reflecting on these questions, you can gain a deeper understanding of what matters most to you and how your values and beliefs shape your identity.

Understand your emotions and motivations

Pay attention to your thoughts, feelings, and actions. Ask yourself why you feel a certain way or why you are motivated to do something. Gaining insight into who you are and can be a powerful tool for gaining insight into your identity. Here's an example of how you might apply this approach:

Let's say you're feeling anxious about an upcoming job interview. Rather than simply ignoring or trying to push aside the feeling, take a moment to reflect on it. Ask yourself:

- Why am I feeling anxious?
- What thoughts or beliefs might be contributing to this feeling?
- Have I felt this way before in similar situations? If so, what was different then?
- What can I do to address or manage my anxiety healthily?

By paying attention to your thoughts, feelings, and actions, you can

The Root of Who You Are

start to uncover deeper patterns and motivations within yourself. You might discover that you tend to feel anxious in situations where you perceive a risk of failure, or that you have a deep-seated belief that success is necessary for your self-worth. With this awareness, you can begin to challenge and reframe these beliefs or develop strategies for coping with anxiety.

Similarly, by reflecting on what motivates you in different areas of your life, you can gain insight into your values and priorities. You might ask yourself:

- What drives me to succeed in my career, hobbies, and/or relationships?
- What brings me a sense of fulfillment or purpose?
- What values or beliefs underlie my goals and aspirations?

When you understand your emotions and motivations in this way, you can start to develop a clearer sense of your authentic self and what matters most to you.

Explore your interests and passions

Take time to discover what you enjoy doing and what you are passionate about. Your interests and passions can be a reflection of your identity and can help you understand what makes you unique.

Let's say you're feeling a bit lost and unsure of who you are. Take some time to think about what activities, hobbies, or topics excite you or bring you joy. Maybe you've always loved photography but haven't picked up a camera in years, or maybe you've been curious about a particular type of music but haven't explored it further.

Take the time to explore these interests in depth. Attend a photography class or workshop, or listen to music from a new genre or culture. Reflect on how these experiences make you feel and what they might say about your identity.

> Take time to discover what you enjoy doing and what you are passionate about.

You might discover that you love photography because it allows you to capture and share moments of beauty and connection, or that you're drawn to music that reflects your cultural heritage or speaks to your values and beliefs.

By exploring your interests and passions in this way, you can gain a deeper understanding of what makes you unique.

Practice self-care. Taking care of your physical and mental health can help you connect with the core of who you are. Make time for activities that nourish your soul and allow you to recharge.

Take a moment to think about what activities or practices help you feel grounded and rejuvenated. Maybe you enjoy taking long walks in nature, practicing yoga, or spending time with close friends.

The Root of Who You Are

Commit to prioritizing these activities in your life, even if it means saying no to other obligations or responsibilities. Carve out time in your schedule for the things that help you feel more connected to your authentic self.

As you engage in these self-care practices, pay attention to how they make you feel. Do they bring you a sense of calm and relaxation? Do they help you connect with your emotions or your sense of purpose? Reflect on these experiences and use them as a guide for making further changes or adjustments in your life.

Prioritize yourself and build a stronger and more fulfilling sense of identity. You'll be better equipped for trials and dificulties.

Then you can be open to opportunities with clarity and confidence.

Remember that getting to know yourself is a lifelong process, and it's okay to not have all the answers right away. Be patient, kind, and curious with yourself as you explore who you are and what makes you unique.

Looking back now, I realize that my stutter has given me a unique perspective of the world. It has forced me to slow down and think carefully about my word choice, and it has taught me the importance of patience and perseverance.

And while I may never completely overcome my stutter, I know that it is a part of who I am.

<u>Affirmation</u>

I am honest with myself.

I hold myself accountable.

Everything is aligning in my life.

I am focused and disciplined.

Chapter 2

Hidden Pain

"Like roots of a tree, some things are hidden deep beneath. You have to dig deeper to find them."
—Lailah Gifty Akita

Walking in the park and being amongst the trees had always been a place of refuge for me. The familiarity of the trails and the hum of the fluorescent sunlight felt comforting in a way. But on this particular day, as I walked with my daughter, I felt anything but comforted.

I was overweight, depressed, and had just gotten out of a relationship with the man I thought I was going to spend the rest of my life with. And to make matters worse, I found myself a new mother with no job and no prospects. Applying for food stamps was just another reminder of how far I had fallen.

Y.O.U.

As I grabbed the Coca Cola out of the vending machine at the food stamp office, my heart sank. The lid was covered in dust, a clear indication it had been in the machine for a long time. I felt like I was at an all-time low, and the weight of my struggles felt crushing.

> *I knew that I had been neglecting my own health and happiness for far too long and that it was time to take action.*

But at that moment, God stirred something in me. I realized that I couldn't continue living my life the same. Choking back tears, I managed to get a few sips of the coke before I put it in my bag. Sitting in the waiting room, I knew needed to make a change. I began reflecting on the areas of my life that were not going right—my health, my relationships, my career—and realized that they were all connected.

I had been neglecting my own health and happiness for far too long and that it was time to take action. I started to make small changes—walking more, eating healthier, and reconnecting with old friends. And as I did, I had a sense of hope that I hadn't felt in a long time.

That moment in the food stamp office was a turning point in my life. It was the moment when I decided to dig deeper, confront my hidden pain and suffering, and start making the changes necessary to create the life I wanted for myself and my daughter.

Anthony J. D'Angelo's, author of *The College Blue Book* said, "When solving problems, dig at the root instead of hacking at the leaves," which stands as a central guiding principle in life. I've learned that it's important to focus on the root cause of a problem rather than merely treating its symptoms.

As I embarked on healing and improving my life, I realized that I had been spending far too much time picking at the leaves of my problems without ever getting to the root of them.

For years, stuttering had been a constant source of frustration and embarrassment. I spent countless hours trying to fix my speech by practicing various techniques and seeking out different treatments, but nothing seemed to work. I felt like I was constantly hacking away at the leaves of my problem without making any progress.

My stuttering wasn't the real problem. It was the shame that I had attached to it that was holding me back. I had internalized the belief that my stuttering made me less capable and less worthy than those who didn't stutter. I was so focused on trying to fix my speech that I didn't realize I needed to address the negative beliefs that were fueling my insecurity.

Self-Reflection

Through self-reflection, I was able to get to the root of my problem and start healing from the inside out. I learned to accept my stutter as a part of who I am and to let go of the shame and fear that had been holding me back. By focusing on the root of my problem, I was

Y.O.U.

able to experience wholeness and fullness in life that I never thought was possible.

Moving forward, I hope you will learn to focus on the root of their problems rather than getting bogged down in the symptoms. Whether it's a physical ailment, an emotional struggle, or a mental challenge, it's important to dig deep and address the underlying beliefs and emotions that are driving the problem. Only then can you truly experience healing and growth.

Focus on the Root

Have you ever found yourself fixating on something about yourself that you perceive as a flaw, even though no one else seems to care or notice? We all have insecurities that can hold us back from living our best lives. Perhaps it's a failed relationship, a toxic friendship, or a health issue that you can't seem to shake.

Everything we face has a root cause, and until we address that root cause, we will continue to struggle with the symptoms.

You can begin working on those things when you start digging deeper and uncovering the root causes of your pain. As you continue reading, think on the areas you want to change. Then start looking back at how yourr life is being impacted by those things. Sometimes it's the circumstances, but a lot of times, we aren't foucsed on the root that created the results.

Hidden Pain

Imagine you have a garden that's filled with weeds. If you were to remove them with a lawnmower, you might be able to get rid of them temporarily. However, the weeds will inevitably grow back, as the root of the problem has not been addressed. On the other hand, if you were to remove the weed from the root, the problem would be solved long-term. It's the same with our lives. Everything we face has a root cause, and until we address that root cause, we will continue to struggle with the symptoms. Think of it as treating the source of the problem, rather than just the symptoms.

The following list provides some examples of leaves and roots:

LEAVES (EFFECT)	**ROOTS (CAUSE)**
Low self-confidence	Setbacks with being overweight
Low income	Mindset that repels money
Emotional eating	Using food for comfort
Procrastination	Fear of failure
Emptiness	Lack of self-love

As we dive into these issues, it's important to remember that healing is a process. It takes time, patience, and self-compassion. By working towards addressing the root cause of our pain, we can begin to live a more fulfilling and authentic life.

As I write this, I am reminded of my struggles with procrastination. Just last week, I found myself rewashing the same load of laundry three times, all while a deadline for this chapter weighed heavily on my mind. My editor had advised me to write for just fifteen to thirty minutes a day, but I struggled to heed her advice. The truth was, my procrastination was rooted in something much bigger than my aversion to writing for a few minutes each day. It was rooted in fear. Fear of failure . Fearl of judgment. It was keeping me stuck.

Through my own experiences and those of others, I have come to realize that procrastination is often a symptom of a deeper issue. It could be a lack of motivation, fear of failure, or even a sense of overwhelm due to other responsibilities. Addressing these underlying causes is the only way to truly overcome procrastination.

Similarly, many self-help books and gurus offer simplistic solutions that fail to address the root causes of our struggles. Telling ourselves that we are the best in the world or that we love doing a task may provide a momentary boost, but it is not a sustainable solution. We must be willing to confront our fears and insecurities and address the underlying issues that are holding us back from achieving our goals. Only then can we create lasting change.

Delayed Gratification

It's natural to want immediate results and to deal with the effects of our problems rather than tackle the root causes. But this approach is limited and won't lead to lasting change.

This is something I experienced firsthand in my journey to overcome stuttering. I saw a speech pathologist and a neurologist,

Hidden Pain

but while their interventions helped, they didn't address the root cause of my stuttering. It wasn't until I faced my fear of speaking in front of people head-on that I started to make real progress.

Similarly, if you struggle with low self-confidence, using techniques like positive self-talk can help in the short term, but they won't solve the underlying problem. To really increase your self-confidence, you

> *When you understand yourself better, you can make conscious choices that align with your values and goals.*

need to understand why you lack it in the first place. This can be a scary process, but it's an essential part of self-mastery, which is the goal of getting to the core of who you are.

Delayed gratification is a key aspect of evolution. It's about sacrificing short-term pleasure for long-term gain. When you tackle the root causes of your problems, you may not see immediate results, but the changes you make will be lasting. This requires patience, persistence, and a willingness to face uncomfortable truths about yourself.

Imagine someone who has struggled with self-worth due to negative comments about their appearance. They may neglect their health, believing they were undeserving of feeling good about themselves. Upon realizing this root issue and acknowledging that they were self-sabotaging their own success, they made a conscious decision to stop the harmful behavior. Instead of seeking quick fixes for weight loss or appearance, they focused on sustainable lifestyle changes and prioritized their well-being.

Over time, as they nurtured both their physical and emotional health, they experienced significant improvements in their overall wellness and self-esteem.So, don't be afraid to dig deeper into the root causes of your problems. It may be a difficult journey, but it's one that will ultimately lead to greater self-awareness and personal growth.

One Size Doesn't Fit All

You may be wondering what this looks like. Before you try to do this, realize that it's not a one-size-fits-all—meaning you aren't going to uncover one thing and get to the root of the issue. You're only going to get to the cause that will lead to the root. It's many effects, many causes, and one root cause (or a few, depending on the situation).

Meaning it's not: Effect → Cause.

It's: Effect → Cause #6 → Cause #5 → Cause #4 → Cause #3 → Cause #2 → Root Cause.

Whether something is a cause or an effect is relative. For example, a cause of an effect is a cause, but this very cause can be the effect of a preceding cause. Cause #4 is the cause of Cause #5. However, Cause #4 is the effect of Cause #3.

Obviously, the best-case scenario is to dig out the root cause of every effect to create the maximum change. However, this can be

Hidden Pain

difficult especially since it involves drilling deep into the problem, being aware of all possible causes and effects extending between reality and your mind, and (oftentimes) digging into the root of your pain.

It's very common to conclude that a particular cause is the root cause, especially if you're not clear on what makes up the entire spectrum of cause

> *The answer doesn't lie outside; it lies within you.*

and effect. Sometimes you may simply run into a dead end because you can't think of any preceding cause—and because I couldn't get rid of stuttering, I came to a dead end. Instead of giving up and turning around, however, I began a journey on an unbeaten path of learning who I was without founding my identity on how I spoke.

Sometimes we find ourselves in situations where we are struggling to understand why we feel the way we do, why we keep making the same mistakes, or why we keep experiencing the same negative outcomes. It can be frustrating and overwhelming, but there are ways to find the root cause of these issues.

Here are some tips to help you find the effect/root causes:

1. Look inward: The root cause is internal, not external. It's always something about us that's causing the issue, whether it's our outlook, beliefs, personality, choices, behavior, or even our past. The answer doesn't lie outside; it lies within you. The deeper you go, the closer you get to the root.

2. Identify patterns: Look for the common denominator of the problems you face. Identify situations when this problem tends to surface, put them side by side, and analyze them. Look for the common denominator in these situations. For example, you may discover that you are always getting into bad relationships because you feel lonely. While this may not be the root cause (e.g., loneliness can be caused by other things such as lack of self-love), it's a possible link to the root cause.
3. Keep questioning: Never assume that something is the final root cause. Keep asking why and digging into it. You'll know something is a root cause when it gives you an "aha" moment and makes you see the situation in a different light.
4. Challenge your beliefs: Often, what we think is normal may not be a norm. For example, we may think that it's normal to feel low self-confidence, but is it true? We may think that it's normal to be angry and feel ticked, but is it true? Challenge what you write and look for contrasting examples and alternative ways of looking at something. This may help you break into the next level.
5. Increase self-awareness: Uncovering the root makes you more aware. Instead of looking at the leaves and branches, look deeper beneath the surface. You will start to see the link between cause and effect and gain a better understanding of yourself. Remember, your strength is in the roots!

Hidden Pain

It can be overwhelming to try to understand the reasons behind everything, so it's best to start with the problems you're currently facing. What obstacles are you encountering in your goals? What negative patterns, bad habits, or issues do you want to tackle? Choose one and start working to uncover the root cause. By doing so, you can make lasting changes instead of continually facing the same problem.

As you focus on finding the root cause, you'll begin to see the cause-and-effect relationship in many situations. This can lead to significant improvements in your life, breaking you free from harmful patterns and behaviors.

God showed me others who experienced similar things I did. Steve Harvey is a well-known comedian, TV host, and author, who has achieved great success in the entertainment industry. However, many people may not know that he stuttered severely in his early years.

As a child, Steve struggled with stuttering, and it greatly impacted his confidence and self-esteem. He was often teased and bullied by his classmates, and he felt like he didn't fit in. While I wasn't bullied or ridiculed, I used basketball as my outlet. Steve found an outlet in humor and began to develop his comedic skills as a way to cope with his stuttering.

Steve also received support and encouragement from his mother, who would often take him to speech therapy sessions and help him practice speaking at home. Through hard work and determination,

Steve was able to overcome his stuttering and develop a successful career in the entertainment industry.

Steve has spoken publicly about his experience with stuttering and has become an advocate for others who may be struggling with the condition. He encourages people to never give up on their dreams, no matter what challenges they may face, and to believe in themselves and their abilities.

Steve's story is a powerful reminder that with perseverance and support, anyone can overcome adversity and achieve great things.

While stuttering is not a self-inflicted pain for me, I have come to realize that I have experienced many other hardships that I could have avoided if I had embraced my true self instead of running away.

Embrace the Pain

Our pain can ultimately become a source of inspiration and strength. It's up to us to harness the incredible power within ourselves and use it to encourage others. Imagine being the catalyst that sparks someone else's dreams and gives them the courage to pursue their heart's desires. That's a powerful gift we can give to the world.

The truth is, struggles are what make us unique and allow us to connect with others on a deeper level. When we face our fears and embrace our vulnerabilities, we allow ourselves to operate in our purpose and make a meaningful impact.

Hidden Pain

It's easy to get caught up in trying to understand everything that happens in our lives, but sometimes, that's just not possible. We must trust

Our pain can ultimately become a source of inspiration and strength.

the journey and have faith that everything will work out in the end. When we do that, we free ourselves from unnecessary stress and worry, and we can focus on living in the present moment and making the most of every opportunity.

Embracing our struggles is a beautiful thing. Returning to the core of who I am meant finding meaning and purpose, not in future desires or predetermined destinies, but in the place where everything began. Sometimes in life, we search for understanding by going back to the beginning—to the seeds from which everything grew. Just as a flower must exist in its seeds before it can bloom, perhaps the end can be found in the beginning.

The dilemma I faced with stuttering was rooted in fear, shame, rejection, and judgment, and the more I operated in fear and shame, the worse my stuttering became. I spent years being unable to move past these emotions, and I convinced myself that I was unworthy, unlovable, and undeserving.

Affirmation

I am proud of myself for overcoming the silent battles no one knew about. The work that I do privately will be evident in every area of my life.

Chapter 3

Facing Your Fears

"The only way fear leaves your being is if you live out the scenario."
—Unknown

I used to be incredibly nervous in social situations, especially when it came to public speaking. Whenever I had to give a presentation or even speak up in a group, my knees would start to tremble, my heart would race, and I would break out in full-body sweat. I felt like I couldn't escape this constant feeling of anxiety, whether I was checking out at the grocery store or trying to order food at a restaurant.

It got to the point where I felt like I had to wear dark colors all the time just to hide the sweat stains on my clothes. I was so consumed by my fear of public speaking that it began to affect every aspect of my life.

Y.O.U.

Operating in fear can have a significant impact on everyday life. Fear can trigger our natural fight-flight-freeze-fawn responses, which can cause physical and emotional changes in the body that can be detrimental if not addressed.

> *Fear can impair our ability to make decisions.*

Here are some ways that operating in fear can impact our daily life:

1. Physical Symptoms: Fear can cause physical symptoms like increased heart rate, sweating, nausea, and muscle tension. If we experience fear frequently, our bodies can become chronically stressed, which can lead to fatigue, headaches, and other physical health problems.
2. Emotional Distress: Fear can also cause emotional distress, such as anxiety, depression, and low self-esteem. Fear can make us feel powerless and out of control, leading to negative self-talk and a feeling of hopelessness.
3. Interpersonal Relationships: Fear can also impact our interpersonal relationships. It can make us defensive, distrustful, and angry, leading to conflicts and misunderstandings with friends, family, and co-workers.
4. Decision-making: Fear can impair our ability to make decisions. When we're operating in fear, we may struggle to think clearly or logically, which can lead to poor decision-making and a feeling of being stuck.

Facing Your Fears

5. Avoidance Behaviors: Fear can also cause us to avoid situations or people that trigger our fear response. This can lead to a limited and constricted life, where we avoid opportunities for growth and self-improvement.

Operating in fear was incredibly challenging until I realized that the only way to overcome my fear was to confront it head-on.

Fear-Based Decisions

Making faith-based decisions is a skill developed over time. The more you practice making decisions in faith, the better you become at it. However, if you continually procrastinate or delay making decisions, you miss out on the opportunity to improve your decision-making ability. Your decision-making muscles need to be exercised regularly to grow stronger, and you need to challenge yourself to make choices frequently.

Unfortunately, some people suffer from decidophobia, which is the irrational fear of making decisions. Even the mere thought of having to make a decision can cause them a significant amount of anxiety. However, if you want to consistently make better decisions, you must learn to confront and overcome any fear you may have of decision-making. Don't let fear prevent you from developing your decision-making skills.

On a personal note, I didn't struggle with decidophobia, but I did find it challenging to manage my emotions and feelings once

I had made a decision. I was talking with someone on the phone and telling them exactly how I felt. I wasn't screaming or yelling, I just spoke my truth and felt proud of myself for deciding to finally speak up. However, I felt bad that the other person was upset and immediately thought about how I could have said it differently. My daughter was sitting in the back seat and she said, "Mom, the truth isn't always nice!" She was right. I've always been the one to try and sugarcoat everything but sometimes you can't and that's ok.

Similarly, some people's insecurities regarding their weight may be reflected in their clothing choices, their appearance, or even their job, indicating that they are seeking validation and acceptance from others. As someone who has struggled with numerous insecurities—including being overweight at one time, I understand the difficulty of feeling self-assured in oneself and one's abilities. Even when things on the outside seemed to be going well for me, I still found myself plagued by self-doubt and negative self-talk.

For me, my insecurities were largely tied to my speech and my fear of not being accepted or liked by others. I would spend hours obsessing over my flaws and comparing myself to others, which only further fueled my feelings of inadequacy.

People-Pleasing

As I became more aware of my decisions, I discovered I was trying to please everyone else. I was giving others the power to dictate my

Facing Your Fears

life. I started to question the decisions I made and whether they were truly aligned with my beliefs or simply made to make someone else happy when it wasn't reciprocated.

I also recognized that my fear of rejection and abandonment was driving my people-pleasing behavior. I was so afraid of being judged or rejected because of my speech that I would do anything to avoid it. However, I realized that by doing so, I was not being true to myself and was sacrificing my own needs and desires for the sake of others.

I remember being in a relationship where I was constantly questioning my actions and motives. I found myself always giving and overcompensating in various areas, just so that my partner wouldn't focus on my speech or use it as an excuse to end the relationship.

There was one particular moment when I had to ask myself *why* I was doing this. I couldn't understand why I kept giving so much when I knew deep down that this person was not doing right by me. It was at that moment that I realized how much my speech was impacting every area of my life. I was so afraid of what my partner thought about my stutter that I overcompensated in other areas to make it seem like it wasn't a big deal.

Looking back, I can see how much this relationship was affecting me. I was constantly second-guessing myself and my actions, and it was taking a toll on my emotional and mental well-being. It wasn't until I started to set boundaries and communicate my needs more effectively that I began to see positive changes in my life.

Y.O.U.

Learning to prioritize my own needs and well-being over others' approval was a difficult but necessary step for me. It allowed me to develop a stronger sense of self and cultivate more authentic and fulfilling relationships in my life. I realized that my worth was not determined by others' opinions of me, and that was a liberating feeling.

In hindsight, I can see how my people-pleasing behavior stemmed from feelings of inadequacy about my speech. I found myself constantly volunteering to pay for things or going out of my way to do something extra nice for someone, just to try and win their approval. This was especially true if I really liked them.

> **Learning to prioritize my own needs and well-being over others' approval was a difficult but necessary step for me.**

On the other hand, I also found myself trying to juggle multiple men at the same time, which I knew deep down wasn't right. I was trying to protect myself from getting hurt, but in the end, it was only causing me more pain and even more anxiety.

I discovered I had a profound sense of self-doubt. I felt insecure and hesitant, especially concerning how others might perceive my speech, fearing they would view me as unintelligent. I was constantly beset by fear and anxiety, which made it difficult for me to form healthy and fulfilling relationships.

However, I also recognized my worth and value wasn't defined by how I spoke. I would work on building my self-confidence and love

Facing Your Fears

and accept myself just the way I was. After all, the more I focused on not speaking well, the more I put my walls up and wasn't being true to myself.

Conquering the Fear of Speaking

In college, I was forced to enroll in a speech class, and like many others, I dreaded the thought of standing in front of the class to deliver a presentation. Of course, my anxiety was different from other people's - they experienced a bit of nervousness, but I would nearly have a breakdown at the thought. It wasn't just the fear of being put on the spot, but also the dread of my speech being delayed or stumbling over my words, especially since nervousness often exacerbated my stuttering.

The mere thought sent shivers down my spine. I was so terrified that I approached my professor, Mr. Wiley, and begged him to let me submit a written assignment in place of the presentation. I was willing to accept a failing grade on the assignment rather than risk the humiliation of public speaking.

Fear became incredibly paralyzing for me and made me focus on the worst-case scenarios. Instead of staying grounded in reality, I found myself overthinking and imagining all the things that could go wrong, such as being laughed at by my peers, running out of time, or not being able to speak at all. The truth was, I had no way of knowing how things would turn out, and my fear prevented me from seeing that.

Y.O.U.

I couldn't avoid public speaking forever. It was a skill that I needed to develop, not just for my college coursework but for my future career as well. I knew that if I continued to let fear control me, it would hold me back from achieving my goals.

> **The future is unpredictable and uncontrollable.**

So, I started putting myself in situations where I had to speak in public, even if it was just in front of a small group of friends. And gradually, I began to feel more confident and comfortable.

The first time I gave a presentation without feeling anxious was a breakthrough moment for me. It wasn't easy, but by facing my fear and living out the scenario, I was able to overcome it. I recognized that I was allowing fear to dictate my decisions, and I was determined to become fearless.

Fear is often based on irrational thoughts and beliefs that we create in our minds. It's easy to get caught up in negative thinking and catastrophizing, but the reality is that most of the time, the things we fear never actually happen. By repeatedly challenging myself and stepping out of my comfort zone, I not only conquered my initial discomfort but also cultivated a new skill set that has proven invaluable both personally and professionally. Embracing these opportunities for growth has unlocked unforeseen possibilities.

The future is unpredictable. Countless variables and factors can influence an outcome, many of which we cannot foresee. It's easy

Facing Your Fears

to get caught up in negative self-talk and assume what others may be thinking about us, but this only feeds into our insecurities and holds us back.

I used to struggle with this myself, feeling like I could read people's minds and anticipate their negative thoughts about me. It took me a while to realize that this type of thinking was not serving me well. Instead, I started focusing on positive affirmations and filling my mind, body, and soul with uplifting thoughts and actions.

I can't control what others think, but I can control my thoughts and actions. By consistently feeding myself positive reinforcements, I built resilience and a better mindset. I had to focus on what I can control and let go of anything that doesn't serve me.

Philippians 4:8 says, "Finally, brothers, whatever is true, whatever is honorable, whatever is just, whatever is pure, whatever is lovely, whatever is commendable if there is any excellence, if there is anything worthy of praise, think about these things."

Our thoughts can quickly begin to spiral into negativity—especially when we focus on all the potential negative outcomes. However, Philippians 4:8 reminds us to shift our focus toward positive and uplifting thoughts. By dwelling on what is true, honorable, just, pure, lovely, commendable, excellent, and praiseworthy, we can redirect our thoughts away from fear and towards a mindset of courage and strength.

When I became intentional about maintaining positive and uplifting thoughts, I discovered it significantly improved my emotional resilience and daily interactions.. The verse Paul wrote encourages us to cultivate a positive mindset that will help us navigate difficult situations with determination. So, when facing fears, let us choose to fix our thoughts on what is good and true, and trust that with God's help, we can overcome any obstacle.

Facing Every Area of Resistance

Change often involves venturing into unfamiliar territory, which can be scary. It's natural to feel hesitant when we're not sure what to expect. To overcome this fear, try to gather as much information as you can about the change and visualize how it might play out. Focus on the potential benefits rather than the risks.

God spoke to me and shared that fear stood for, "Face every area of resistance!" He showed me that by facing every area of resistance, I could break through limiting beliefs and behaviors and unlock my full potential for growth and success. And you can too!

It requires a willingness to step outside of our comfort zones, take risks, and embrace new experiences, but the rewards can be significant in terms of personal and professional fulfillment. Wherever I felt a wall or something was holding me back, I began pushing through it—starting with going skydiving!

Facing Your Fears

When I arrived at the venue, I could feel the excitement building in my chest. I saw the planes lined up on the runway, and the instructors bustling around, preparing for their next jump. I checked in and signed my waiver, trying to ignore the little voice in my head telling me to turn back. Along with my daughter who was like, "Mommy no, I don't want you to jump out of an airplane."

Next, I was taken through a training session where the instructors went over everything from how to exit the plane to how to control my body during free fall. They showed me how to wear the jumpsuit, harness, and helmet, and went over the emergency procedures, just in case.

As the time drew closer for my jump, I started to feel nervous. I kept checking and rechecking my equipment, hoping that everything was secure and that I wouldn't mess up. I tried to calm myself by reminding myself of all the safety precautions I had gone over in the training session. *I can do this.* I am doing this!

Finally, it was time to board the plane. I took a deep breath and climbed aboard, finding my seat and settling in. I could hear the hum of the engines as the plane started to taxi down the runway. My heart beat faster and faster as I felt the plane start to lift off the ground.

> *I was scared, but I knew I had to do this.*

My mind raced with anticipation. As we ascended higher and higher, the view from the window became more and more breathtaking. The green fields and trees below looked so small. I could feel the tension building in my body. I tried to focus on the beautiful scenery outside the window, hoping it would distract me from my fears.

As the plane reached the required altitude, the instructor strapped me onto him, and we made our way to the open door of the plane. "You're first," he said.

Suddenly, everything around me seemed to slow down. I thought since I got on last, I would jump last. My mind was in overdrive, my heart was pounding in my chest, and my stomach was doing somersaults. I was scared, but I knew I had to do this.

The instructor gave me the final instructions, and before I knew it, we were free-falling. The sensation was like nothing I had ever felt before. The wind rushing past me, the noise of the air whistling in my ears, and the incredible feeling of weightlessness was all overwhelming. For a few seconds, I felt like I was flying, soaring through the sky like a bird—with no care or worries in the world.

As we began to slow down, the instructor deployed the parachute, and we started to glide down to the ground. The view from above was simply stunning. The landscape stretched out before me in all directions, and I felt like I could see for miles.

When we landed, I was filled with a sense of accomplishment and pride. I had faced my fear and conquered it.

Facing Your Fears

Comfort and Control

As humans, we are inclined to seek comfort and *control* in our lives. We prefer a sense of predictability and stability, which can make change feel uncomfortable. This desire for control can sometimes make us feel like we are losing control when faced with change, leading to resistance.

Similarly, we tend to be creatures of habit and get comfortable with our routines, even if we're not happy with them. It's easy to become complacent and accept the status quo because it's familiar, rather than taking a risk and making a change. This comfort can lead to resistance towards change, even when it could lead to positive outcomes.

It's essential to identify where the fear of change is coming from and address it. For example, if the fear is rooted in the loss of control, finding ways to take an active role in the change process can help regain a sense of control. Similarly, if the resistance comes from comfort with the status quo, it's important to challenge assumptions and think about how the change could lead to positive outcomes.

> *While it's natural to fear the unknown, it's important not to let that fear hold us back.*

By acknowledging our natural tendencies towards comfort and control, we can better understand why we might be resistant to change and take steps to overcome it. It's important to remember that change is a natural part of life.

While it's natural to fear the unknown, it's important not to let that fear hold us back. Instead, we can take steps to identify where our fear is coming from and address it. By focusing on the aspects of change that we do have control over and finding ways to make ourselves more comfortable with the unknown, we can overcome our fear and embrace new opportunities for growth and improvement.

Avoiding Repetitive Failures

After my former relationship ended, I found myself struggling with the fear of getting into a new relationship. That relationship had been a significant part of my life, and I had invested a lot of time and emotions into it. When it ended, I felt like a part of me was missing, and I was hesitant to open myself up to the possibility of being hurt again.

I was afraid of repeating the same mistakes and making the same choices that had led to the end of my previous relationship. I feared that I would never be able to find someone who would love and accept me for who I was. These fears made it difficult for me to trust others and to be vulnerable in future relationships.

I sought support from my friends and family and began engaging in activities that brought me joy and fulfillment. I also started to reflect on my past relationship and learned valuable lessons that helped me become more self-aware.

Facing Your Fears

Gradually, my fear of getting into a new relationship started to fade away, and I became more open to the idea of meeting someone new. While there were still moments of hesitation and doubt, I learned to trust myself and my instincts. Today, I am in a healthy and loving relationship, and I am grateful for the journey that led me here.

Getting to the root of my fears was a crucial step toward self-acceptance. It allowed me to finally confront and let go of the negative beliefs that had been holding me back for so long.

The root causes of my insecurities were largely tied to past experiences of rejection and self-criticism related to my stutter—many of which I created myself. Once I was able to understand the origins of my fears, I could begin to challenge and reframe them.

It wasn't an easy process, but as I worked through my issues and began to build my self-confidence, I found that I was able to let go of the past and embrace the present with more openness and positivity. I no longer felt defined or limited by my past. Instead, I was able to approach relationships and other areas of my life with greater authenticity and freedom.

While there will always be moments of uncertainty, I am now equipped with the resources to navigate them effectively. My past experiences have taught me not to allow them to dictate my future.

Y.O.U.

I want to leave you with some of the tools that helped me when I was in my darkest moments:

1. Practice self-compassion: Treat yourself with the same kindness and compassion that you would offer to a good friend. Acknowledge your struggles and challenges, but also remind yourself of your strengths and positive qualities.
2. Set small, achievable goals: Setting small, achievable goals can help build confidence and provide a sense of accomplishment. Focus on taking small steps toward your goals, rather than trying to tackle everything at once.
3. Surround yourself with supportive people: Seek out relationships and connections with people who are supportive and affirming. Having a positive support network can help bolster your self-confidence and provide encouragement when you're feeling doubtful.
4. Practice mindfulness and self-reflection: Take time to check in with yourself regularly, and incorporate techniques like meditation, getting into the Bible, and listening to a sermon.

These tools can help you become more aware of your thoughts and emotions, and provide a sense of clarity and perspective so you can move forward.

Affirmation

I trust my intuition.

I can make great decisions.

I am my own validation.

Chapter 4

Cultivating Courage and Strength

"Be strong and courageous. Do not be terrified: do not be discouraged, for the Lord, your God, will be with you wherever you go."
—Joshua 1:9

Courage and strength are not just words to me; they are a way of life. As women, we are often told to be gentle, to be meek, to be quiet. But I am here to tell you that there is power in being strong, in being bold, in being fearless.

These qualities are for the everyday battles we face as women. Whether it's fighting for equal pay at work, raising children on our own, or battling an illness, we must tap into the strength and courage within us to overcome these obstacles.

Y.O.U.

Courage is within each of us; however, we have to do the work and figure out what it is that drives us, and what keeps us pushing forward, even when the odds are against us.

For me, it's my faith in God. It's knowing that I am not alone, that there is a higher power guiding me and giving me the strength to face whatever comes my way. When I tap into my relationship with God, when I truly believe it in my heart, that's when my courage is cultivated.

So my challenge to you today, my sisters, is to find that thing that drives you, that thing that gives you the strength to keep going. It may be your faith, it may be your family, or it may be your dreams and aspirations.

Have you ever had a moment where your body just felt like it couldn't go on any longer? Where you felt chills running up your arms and uncertainty taking over your entire being? I know I have. In fact, I experienced this feeling every day leading up to one particular moment in my life—one that I fought to have.

I had been working out with a personal trainer for two years, putting in over a hundred hours at the gym. I would wake up at 4 a.m., work out, rush to drop off my daughter at daycare, head to work, and pray that I made it there safe and on time.

After work, I would battle through traffic, pick up my daughter, spend a few moments with her, and then head back to the gym for another workout.

Cultivating Courage and Strength

As mothers, we sacrifice for our children, and this was one I was willing to make for both of us. I knew that if I could get my physical body back in shape, it would help my spiritual and financial life fall back into place, making me a better woman and mom overall. And let me tell you, there were days when I felt like I had nothing left to give. Days when I was running on fumes, when my body was tired, and my spirit was weak.

But I kept going, I kept pushing forward, and I kept praying. Praying for that third wind, praying for the strength to pick up my daughter from daycare and be present with her, even if it was just for a few moments.

And you know what? God answered those prayers. He gave me the strength to keep going, to keep pushing forward, and to keep being the best mother I could be.

Step Out of Your Comfort Zone

One day, everything seemed to collapse around me, suffocating me under a weight I couldn't bear. It was as if I had hit a wall, a barrier formed by my own relentless grip of anxiety. I had been focusing on my health. An opportunity to compete in a fitness competition presented itself to me, and I was eager to push myself beyond my limits. I knew I was ready to compete, but as I prepared to take that first step. Even if I was going to fall on my face.

Here's the thing, fear is not a sign to stop. Fear is a sign that you are on the verge of doing something great. So even though every part of my body was telling me to give up, I took that step anyway.

> *Fear is a sign that you are on the verge of doing something great.*

And you know what? All of the hard work I had put in up until that point had prepared me for that moment. I may have felt like I was going to fall on my face, but instead, I soared.

When I registered for my first bikini fitness competition, excitement and anticipation were real, but so was the fear. As I was about to hit that stage, I couldn't help but think, *"Why did you sign up for this, girl? Are you crazy?"*

The negative self-talk started to creep in, but I knew I couldn't let it consume me. I had to remind myself that I was not alone. God was with me every step of the way, and I was bold and courageous—I was taking action in the face of fear. And let me tell you, fear was definitely present that day. But instead of operating in fear, I decided to flip the script and embrace a new definition of fear.

As I mentioned previously, God had defined F.E.A.R. for me as: "Face Every Area of Resistance." And that day, I decided to embrace it in a new way. When you allow self-doubt to dictate your actions, you risk stagnation. By succumbing to fear and avoiding areas of resistance, you may inadvertently surrender the dreams entrusted to you by God, leaving them to be fulfilled by another.

Cultivating Courage and Strength

Everything you want is on the other side of your fears. So don't let fear stop you from going after what you truly desire. I'm a witness that life will transform before your very eyes!

It's not just about facing resistance in our careers or our relationships. It's about facing resistance in every area of our lives. Difficulties aren't isolated occurrences but rather interconnected elements woven into the fabric of our existence. Whether it's our health, our finances, or our personal growth, there will always be resistance. But it's how we respond to that resistance that makes all the difference.

Instead of running away from our problems or giving up when things get tough, if you find yourself backed into a corner and want to give up, don't do it just yet! Are you ready to commit to pushing past fear, or will you let it define you.

Use Your Power

Life has a way of taking us on a path that we never imagined. But here's the thing, when we start walking like we rule the world, we attract the very things that we need to fulfill our destiny.

As I walk into a room to give a speech or attend a networking event, I can't help but hear Beyonce's voice in my head saying, "Who runs the world? *Girls!*" And you know what? It's true. Women run the world. We have the power to make a difference and create the life we want.

Y.O.U.

> *But here's the thing, when we start walking like we rule the world, we attract the very things that we need to fulfill our destiny.*

Sometimes, we're unsure of our destination, but it's crucial to figure it out. If you don't, you'll find yourself drifting, getting further away from where you need to be. Remember, every step either brings you closer to your goals or takes you further away. We have to know where we're not going and be willing to do whatever it takes to avoid going back to those dark places of depression and struggle.

I remember sitting in that food stamp office, feeling ashamed and humiliated as a rude lady looked down on me. But I knew that wasn't where I was meant to be. I knew that I had a purpose and a destiny to fulfill, and I was determined to make it happen.

Let me paint you a picture. Imagine waking up every morning feeling defeated, your heart heavy with pain, and your mind consumed with toxic thoughts about yourself. You cry yourself to sleep every night and indulge in unhealthy eating habits. Your self-esteem is at an all-time low, and you're weighed down by the burden of feeling unattractive and unworthy. That was my reality at that time, and if you're reading this, perhaps it's yours too. But let me tell you something, it doesn't have to be this way. There is a way out, and I'm here to share with you what I did to escape that dark place and find my way back to the light.

Cultivating Courage and Strength

I know you're curious as to how I escaped that dark place where tears were my constant companion, where I indulged in any food that caught my fancy, and where I convinced myself of my unattractiveness while weighing two-hundred pounds. Well, my friend, get ready to take out your notepad for this one!

Every single day, I tuned in to "The Word Network." For those who may be unfamiliar, it's a Christian network that broadcasts pastoral sermons and plays uplifting gospel and Christian music. From 8-9 a.m., I would tune in to T.D. Jakes. From 9-10 a.m., it was Joyce Meyer; and whoever came on next, as long as they spoke to my spirit, I would listen in. I firmly believe that building a personal relationship with God is crucial. While I had grown up in the church and knew who God was, it wasn't until I had no one else to turn to but Him that I truly got to know Him.

There comes a point in your life where you begin to live for an audience of one–Him! Every morning, I would jot down notes, and day by day, in every single way, I grew stronger .

What Are You Feeding Your Future?

Joyce Meyer preached a message and shared, "What you feed longest becomes strongest." That statement hit me like a ton of bricks because it was true. When you nourish your spirit with the word of God, you become stronger in that area. It's just like working out your physical body; the longer you exercise, the stronger you become, and the more confident you are in your body. Do you see how everything works together?

I challenge you to start feeding your spiritual self every day. It's time to take action, my friend. You may not have the luxury of an entire morning dedicated to listening to sermons, but that's okay. Start somewhere. Maybe you have thirty minutes on your way to work, so why not use that time to listen to a podcast that feeds your spirit? Find something that ignites a fire within you and makes you feel alive.

> **Find something that ignites a fire within you and makes you feel alive.**

It's time to prioritize your spiritual well-being, even if it's just for a few minutes a day. Take ten minutes to journal your thoughts and feelings or write a gratitude list. You'd be surprised at how much a little bit of reflection and gratitude can strengthen you.

This is not about perfection or living up to someone else's expectations. It's about doing something every day that nourishes your soul. It's about finding what works for you and sticking to it.

Not everyone will understand your journey to becoming your best self, and that's okay. It can be lonely. You may even have to have some tough conversations with the people you love.

One morning my mama walked into the living room and asked me, "Are you going to church today?"

Cultivating Courage and Strength

I looked at her and said, "Nope."

Let me tell you, the look on her face was priceless! She went on to tell me that watching OWN all day wouldn't help me grow spiritually and that I needed to come to church.

But here's the thing, sis: You know yourself better than anyone else. You know what you need to do in order to become the best version of yourself.

My mom has seven sisters, and they all went to the same church. My grandma was a missionary in the church, and my great-grandfather was even the pastor at one point. So when I say our roots run deep, I mean it! I had been sitting on a pew since I was in the womb.

> *You have to follow your own path, even if it means going against the expectations of those closest to you.*

Even with all that history and tradition, I couldn't shake the feeling that I needed something different. I felt like I needed more than just the sermons and hymns that I had grown up with. And that's when Oprah entered the picture. The guests Oprah had on her show were speaking to my soul. Every guest she brought on was feeding me spiritually, from Deepak Chopra to Gary Zukav to Byron Pitts, and so many more. And yet, my mama just didn't understand why I wasn't going to church with her.

You have to follow your own path, even if it means going against the expectations of those closest to you. It takes courage to break away from tradition and do something different, but it's worth it if it means discovering your true self.

Sis, let me tell you, I didn't know how to help my mama understand. Every Sunday, without fail, we would have the same conversation.

"Are you going to church today?" she would ask, and I would say no.

Then she would give me that look, *that look* that only a mama can give. But I didn't feel the need to explain myself to her—or anyone else for that matter. I was on a journey, a journey to find God on a deeper level within myself.

The different people I listened to taught me there's something greater within me, something that's more powerful than anything in this world. As 1 John 4:4 says, "Greater is he that is within you, than he that is within the world."

So even though my mama didn't understand, I kept going. I kept searching. I kept seeking. And eventually, I found what I was looking for. I established an even better relationship with God for myself, and it changed everything.

Watching OWN and other faith messages every morning for a year made me realize: It's only when you stop moving that you truly recieve the strength and courage you need.

Affirmation

I see myself reaching my best potential and abilities.

I have no choice but to be amazing.

I am destined for greatness.

Chapter 5

Breaking Free from Doubt

"Doubt your doubts before you doubt your faith."
—Dieter F. Uchtdorf

Do you ever find yourself grappling with self-doubt? That little nagging voice that whispers, "You're not good enough," "You're not worthy," or "You don't have what it takes." It's a common struggle that we face as we journey through life, but we must not let it hinder us from living our best and most fulfilling lives.

When we doubt ourselves, our minds become suspended in a state of indecision, uncertain of which path to take. We find ourselves stuck between contradictory propositions, unable to be certain of anything. And it's not just a mental battle.

Doubt seeps into our emotions, too, causing us to waver between belief and unbelief. It can bring about feelings of distrust, and a lack of conviction in our actions, motives, and decisions.

Y.O.U.

However, doubt doesn't have to be a permanent companion. It's possible to overcome it and step into a life of purpose and fulfillment. It starts with acknowledging that doubt is a normal part of the human experience and that you're not alone in your struggles.

Then, take some time to identify the root of your doubts. Is it a fear of failure? A lack of confidence in your abilities? Once you've pinpointed the source, begin challenging those doubts with affirmations of your worth and value.

I want you to know that you are not alone in your struggles. Life can be tough, and sometimes it feels like the challenges we face are too much to bear.

I was weighed down by my circumstances. I was overweight, jobless, a new mother, no husband to lean on, and had moved back in with my mom. It felt like I was taking one step forward and two steps back. The weight of it all slowly started to get heavier.

> But even in the midst of my darkest moments, I held on to the hope that things would get better.

But even in the midst of my darkest moments, I held on to the hope that things would get better. Have you ever felt like the weight of the world was on your shoulders, and there was nothing you could do to escape it? This was exactly how I felt. I was completely tapped out, with no idea how to move forward.

Breaking Free from Doubt

Allow me to take you back to that dark time in my life. A time when every night felt like a battle, and every morning felt like a defeat.

As I lay in bed, my mind would race with thoughts of all the things that had gone wrong in my life. The weight of my circumstances was like an anchor, dragging me down deeper and deeper into despair.

And then the tears would come. Hot, salty tears flowed down my cheeks and soaked my pillow. I would cry until my throat was raw and my eyes were swollen shut.

In the midst of my own pain, the cries of my baby became my saving grace. Her little voice was a reminder that I couldn't give up, that I had to keep fighting.

Instead of listening to the voice of doubt, God used my daughter to push me. She pushed me to let go. Doubt would sneak up on me when I least expected it. But every time it did, I reminded myself of how far I had come, and how much more I was capable of achieving.

So I would wipe away my tears, take a deep breath, and go to her. I would hold her close and feel her little body snuggle into mine, and for a moment, everything else would fade away.

There were days when I summoned every ounce of strength to rise from bed, battling through the heaviness. Unbeknownst to me, I was facing postpartum depression, compounded by the challenges of being a new single mom. The life I had envisioned was slipping away, and progress felt painfully slow, like a turtle on a lazy day. But you know what? I kept going, even when it felt like I was barely moving forward. I knew that progress, no matter how slow, was still progress.

It was during those dark moments that I realized that I was meant for more than the life I was living. In fact, I wasn't living. At times, I was just existing. I had worked too hard to give up now. So I started to replay all of my accomplishments over and over in my head, reminding myself of how great I had been and still was. And with each small victory, my confidence grew. So if you're feeling like your progress is moving at a snail's pace, just remember that slow and steady wins the race.

It's okay to feel overwhelmed or unsure of what to do next. Just don't stay there! Remember that you are meant for more than the difficulties you're facing. Those difficult moments were the catalyst for my growth.

If you're struggling with doubt, I encourage you to let it go. Release it like a balloon into the sky, and believe in yourself. Take those small steps, and before you know it, you'll look back and realize how far you've come.

Do You Want to be Healed?

"Girl, get up!" Those were the words that echoed in my mind as I listened to Sarah Jakes Roberts' message. I had heard her preach before, but this time her words hit me in a different way.

Breaking Free from Doubt

In her sermon, Sarah talked about the story of the paralyzed man in John 5, who had been lying by the pool of Bethesda for thirty-eight years, waiting for someone to help him into the water when it was stirred. But when Jesus came and asked him if he wanted to be healed, the man's response was not a resounding "Yes!", but rather a list of excuses and complaints.

Jesus asked the man a question that seems so obvious, but is often the hardest one to answer: Do *you* want to be healed? Sometimes, we get so comfortable in our pain that we forget what it feels like to walk. Jesus is asking us the same question today. The same question that was speaking to me so many years ago. Do you want to be healed?

As I listened to her words, I couldn't help but think about how often I had been like that paralyzed man, stuck in my own thoughts, waiting for someone else to come and rescue me. But Jesus' message to the man was not just to be healed, but also to "pick up your mat and walk" (John 5:8). That message reminded me of what my mother told me in the midst of my brokenness.

> *Do you want to be healed? Sometimes, we get so comfortable in our pain that we forget what it feels like to walk.*

Growing up, my mother had to be the strong one for her six sisters, and she learned to be a fighter. In the midst of my lowest point, I'm grateful for what my mom told me. With heartfelt sincerity, she said, "You have one day to cry and feel sorry for yourself! Then, you have to get up and put yourself back together for your daughter."

She knew what it took to thrive in this world, and she wasn't about to let me give up on myself. As I reflect back, I can't help but be grateful for my mother's tough love. It may have seemed slightly harsh, but she knew what I needed at that time—a wake-up call.

Just like the man with the mat, it's not enough to be healed if we're not willing to take action. We have to pick up our mats and walk. We have to be willing to leave our old ways behind and step into a new life.

And that's the message that I want to share with you. Do you want to be healed? Are you ready to pick up your mat and walk?

When I found myself in a dark place, consumed by self-pity, my mother stepped in with her no-nonsense attitude. My mother emphasized the importance of picking myself up and pressing on.

So I did. The very next day was the day I began my journey toward self-improvement. I began focusing on my physical health. With every workout, every sweat-drenched session, I felt myself getting stronger—not just physically, but mentally and emotionally as well.

To this day, my mother's words reverberate in my mind like a beacon of hope, reminding me that I can rise up out of the trenches of depression. I knew that I couldn't just sit and wait for someone else to rescue me. I had to take action to pick up my mat and walk. With renewed determination, I took a deep breath and stood up.

Through this process, I discovered the transformative power of forgiveness—of releasing the burden of past mistakes and embracing self-acceptance. It was a challenging road, but it led to profound healing. As Taraji P. Henson shared with Oprah, "Forgiveness is a gift you give yourself."

Determination Destroys Doubt

I pray over my mind and speak positive affirmations over myself. I do this because I've come to realize that the thoughts we entertain have a direct impact on our emotional, mental, and even physical well-being.

In fact, becoming aware of your thoughts and the conversations you have with yourself about yourself is one of the most transformative things you can ever do for yourself. As women, we often find ourselves falling prey to the trap of comparison, constantly measuring ourselves against other women and feeling inferior as a result.

But here's the thing, sis, comparison is the thief of joy. It robs us of our confidence and self-assurance, and it plants a seed of self-doubt that, if left unchecked, can grow and manifest in all areas of our lives.

That's why it's crucial that we intentionally guard our minds and take control of our thoughts. We must refuse to entertain negative self-talk and instead choose to speak life-giving words over ourselves.

Y.O.U.

We must declare and believe that we are fearfully and wonderfully made, unique and special in our own way.

I encourage you to make a conscious effort to monitor your thoughts and speak positively over yourself. Remember, your words have power, and as you sow positivity into your mind, you'll begin to see a transformation in your overall outlook on life.

> *I was determined to overcome my fear and reclaim my voice.*

At the tender age of twenty-seven, right after having Aliyah, my mom's words struck me like a bolt of lightning, stirring something deep within me. I was determined to break free from the shackles that had held me captive for far too long and get back into the workforce. The stress of it all had taken its toll on me, causing my stutter to worsen to the point where speaking became a daunting task.

I knew that in order to regain my confidence, I had to put myself in positions where I could speak consistently. So, I started taking small steps, like practicing my speech by placing orders at drive-thru restaurants. I would often get angry at myself for stumbling over my words, but I refused to give up. Instead, I would slow down, take a deep breath, and remind myself that no one was judging me.

This became a daily ritual for me, a conversation I had with myself multiple times throughout the day. I was determined to overcome my fear and reclaim my voice. And with each passing day, I could feel my stutter diminishing.

Searching for Answers

After attending several networking events and indulging in unnecessary food, I had a realization—I needed to take control of my health. I had already consulted with a speech pathologist when I was fresh out of college, but she found nothing wrong with my speech during our sessions. Despite this, I knew something was not right.

As a result, I decided to see a neurologist who ran several tests on my brain. However, to my dismay, he found nothing out of the ordinary. Instead, he suggested that speech anxiety might be the root of the problem. In an effort to alleviate my anxiety, he prescribed me Lexipro, an anxiety medication.

I followed my doctor's instructions and took Lexipro for two months, but I noticed a significant change in myself every time I took the medicine. It was as though I was having an out-of-body sensation.

Everything around me moved at a glacial pace, including myself. I was no longer the vibrant, energetic person I had always been. My natural zest for life was gone.

Simple things like working out, reading, attending networking events, or just conversing with people were no longer appealing to me. I was a walking zombie, trapped in a state of numbness.

Y.O.U.

It became apparent to me that this medication was not the solution to my problem. I knew I needed to find another way to overcome my speech anxiety.

Self-Love

Feeling like something is off in your life can leave you feeling restless and uneasy. It's like being trapped in a cage with no escape, and you hold the key to unlock it, but you don't know where to start. Trust me, I've been there.

> *Self-development begins with being honest with yourself about who you are and who you want to become.*

But let me tell you something that I've learned through my journey of self-discovery: The key to unlocking your destiny is self-love. And not just any kind of love, but the love that God has for us. You see, when you start to truly love yourself, you'll see things in a different light. You'll realize that you are worthy of all the good things in life, and that you deserve happiness.

Self-development begins with being honest with yourself about who you are and who you want to become. You need to face your inner demons and unhealthy patterns. You learn to love yourself despite them. This is unconditional love, just like the love that God has for us.

And let me tell you, self-work isn't a walk in the park. It means forgiving yourself for past mistakes, whether it's having a baby out of wedlock or lying to make yourself look good. It means being honest with yourself and others, even when it hurts.

You are God's Masterpiece

You are a masterpiece, created by the Almighty God with such care and attention to detail that the very thought of you makes His heart swell with love and pride. You are fearfully and wonderfully made, with unique gifts, talents, and purpose woven into the very fabric of your being (Psalm 139:14).

But let's be real, sometimes, it can be hard to see ourselves in that light. We can get so caught up in our flaws that we no longer recognize the reflection in the mirror. That's when we need to fall head over heels in love with ourselves—flaws and all—until our mistakes become mere specks on the canvas of our lives.

Our past doubts and experiences are no match for the power and love of God. We make the oversight of magnifying our struggles, but when we turn our focus to Him, we see that He is infinitely greater than anything we may face or have endured in the past. For years, I let my speech impediment define me. But when I surrendered that struggle to God, I saw that He was in control of it all along. And in that surrender, I found a newfound security, a confidence that was not rooted in my own abilities but in the knowledge that God was in control.

So I encourage you today, sis—ask God to help you see yourself as He sees you. Let His love immerse your heart and mind until you find complete security in your identity in Him. Remember, as Ephesians 2:10 says, "You are God's masterpiece, created anew in Christ Jesus, uniquely fashioned with purpose and worth."

Made in His Image

The memory of when I first heard about being made in God's image escapes me. But as I reflect on those words now, a profound revelation unfolds. If you truly believe that you are made in His image, then you should how perfectly imperfect you are. It's easy to get caught up in the little things that don't really matter, instead of embracing the wonderful creation that God made you to be. But how do you fall in love with yourself? That was the question that plagued me for so long. I had no idea where to begin.

What I did know was that I was created for a purpose. I felt a deep yearning inside of me to do something great, to make a difference in the world. I wanted to follow in the footsteps of Lisa Nichols, the international motivational speaker and founder of Motivating the Masses. Her story resonated with me deeply, as she had also been a single mother on food stamps before becoming a multimillionaire.

I started acknowledging my flaws and accepting them. My imperfections make me unique and beautiful in my own way. I began to focus on how I could use them to make a positive impact in the world.

Breaking Free from Doubt

As I continued on this path, I learned to love myself more and more each day. I started to see myself through God's eyes, to truly begin pursuing my purpose and living a life that glorifies Him.

Craving Clarity

Have you ever experienced those days when our thoughts seem scattered like leaves in the wind? I know I have. It's like having a 'squirrel brain,' where focusing on anything feels nearly impossible. When clarity eludes us, we can become hindered in our progress towards our goals. The inner chaos makes simple tasks insurmountable. Tackling our to-do lists is the last thing we want to do. It's during these times that our inner critic seems loudest, making it tempting to abandon our goals altogether. Or am I the only one?

Cultivating mental clarity is paramount. I make it a daily goal to begin and end my day with a clear mind. One way I achieve this is by writing out my thoughts, organizing them on paper, and gaining perspective on what truly matters.

Journaling and writing down the vision that God has placed in my heart became a roadmap guiding me.

I knew deep down that God had a plan for my life. So, I made a decision to seek His guidance. There were days when I didn't feel like reading my Bible or praying. But I pushed through those moments and continued to nourish my soul.

Y.O.U.

> *I recognized that my imperfections make me unique and beautiful in my own way.*

The prophet Habakkuk wrote, "Write the vision, make it plain on tablets, so he may run who reads it" (Habakkuk 2:2-3). This verse speaks to me because it reminds me that once I write down the vision God has given me and work out the plan, it will surely come to pass.

Writing down my dreams, my fears, and my doubts gave me clarity and direction. I wrote on anything that was close by, whether it was a napkin, a receipt, or an envelope. Taking notes became something I craved every day.

Oh, how I craved clarity! It was as if my soul was yearning for something more, something greater than what I was currently experiencing. And as I continued to feed my spiritual man every day and write down my vision, I began to see more clearly.

I realized that the doubts and fears that had been holding me back were just illusions. They were like a veil that had been clouding my vision, preventing me from seeing the path that God had laid out for me.

But as I wrote down my dreams and desires, I began to see that they were not just wishful thinking. They were real and attainable. And I knew that if I continued to work towards them with faith and determination, I would reach my destiny.

Breaking Free from Doubt

Sis, if you are feeling lost or unsure of your purpose, I urge you to start writing down your vision. Be specific and clear about what you want to achieve. And don't let doubts and fears hold you back. Trust in God's timing and have faith that your vision will come to pass.

Heavenly Father,

I come to you today with a humble heart and ask that you grant me the strength and courage to become secure in my insecurities—both the seen and unseen. Help me to become so secure in myself that I am no longer held back by fear or doubt. May your love and light guide me through any challenges that come my way, and may I always remember that I am worthy and loved just as I am. I trust in your divine plan for my life and ask for your continued guidance and blessings. Thank you for all that you do for me.

In Jesus' name,
Amen.

Affirmation

I believe in my dreams.

I am confident that the desires

of my heart will be fulfilled.

Chapter 6

It's Okay to Pause

"Pausing is not a waste of time. It's an investment in clarity."
— Jennifer Ritchie Payette

Life has a way of teaching us lessons in the most unexpected ways. I know this firsthand, especially after I lost my job and was thrown into the whirlwind of job interviews.

Hoping for some good news, I received a second call back from a potential employer. In my heart, I was convinced that this was the opportunity I had been praying for.

The first interview had gone well, and I remembered how the CFO had struggled with stuttering just like I did. The empathy that I received from the interviewer when I shared my own struggles gave me hope that this job could be mine. But as fate would have it, things didn't quite go according to *my* plans.

Y.O.U.

During the second interview, my stuttering got the best of me, and I struggled to get even a single word out. It was frustrating, and I felt as though I had lost my voice.

The CFO of the company asked me to sing my answers to him. Now, this caught me off guard. Sing my answers? Was he serious? At first, I felt embarrassed.

> *I could have let my speech impediment hold me back, but I chose to embrace it and adapt.*

As I reflect back on that experience, I now understand that it was a necessary lesson in slowing down. You might be wondering: What does singing have to do with stuttering? Well, as it turns out, singing engages a different part of our brain than speaking. This is why many people who stutter when they talk can sing without any problem. It's almost like magic—the words flow effortlessly, and the stutter disappears.

Marilyn Monroe and James Earl Jones were iconic figures who struggled with stuttering in their early years. But they found that they could speak without stuttering when they used a different tone of voice or spoke in a character's voice. For Marilyn, it was her breathy, sultry voice that helped her overcome her stutter, while for James, it was his deep, resonant voice that did the trick.

So when the CFO told me to sing my answers, I understood what he meant. He wasn't trying to be mean or make fun of my stutter.

It's Okay to Pause

He was trying to help me overcome it by tapping into a different part of my brain.

I could have let my speech impediment hold me back, but I chose to embrace it and adapt. Oh, the nerves! Every part of my body was in overdrive, and I could feel the sweat beads forming on my forehead. But even in that moment of intense pressure, I stayed calm and collected.

When I was in that interview, and my speech impediment seemed to have taken over, I could have easily panicked. But instead, I took a deep breath and gave myself a pep talk. *"Just slow down, Alexis,"* I told myself. *"Take a deep breath and collect your thoughts."*

And you know what? It worked. By taking a moment to pause and center myself, I was able to regain my composure and continue with the interview. I learned that sometimes, the best thing we can do in moments of stress is to take a step back and give ourselves the space we need to recharge.

So if you ever find yourself in a nerve-wracking situation, remember to breathe. Take a moment to pause, gather your thoughts, and remind yourself that you are capable of overcoming whatever you are currently experiencing. With practice, you'll find that even the most stressful situations become more manageable, and you'll be able to face them with a more calm and confident demeanor.

In the end, I gained something significant: the confidence to keep going despite my setbacks. That experience taught me that life is not about what happens to us, but how we respond to it. And as long as we keep pushing forward, nothing can stop us from reaching our goals and fulfilling our purpose.

Sometimes the hardest thing to do is to allow things to happen naturally. And this is especially true when it comes to stuttering. When I was struggling with my speech impediment, I would try to force my words out, thinking that if I just pushed hard enough, the stutter would disappear. But as it turned out, this approach only made things worse. I started developing other bad habits, like jerking my head or tapping my foot, anything to try and force the words out.

But then, I had a breakthrough moment. I realized that stuttering is a complex issue that requires patience. I started paying attention to the words that triggered my stuttering, and I tried to use other words in their place. I also learned that it's okay to pause, to take a moment to collect my thoughts and to control my breathing. And you know what? It worked.

As I continued to work on my speech impediment, I started to see parallels in other areas of my life. Sometimes, the best thing we can do is to slow down, to take a step back, and reassess our situation. The greatest breakthroughs come not from pushing harder, but from letting go and allowing things to happen naturally.

> **There is no shame in slowing down to catch our breath.**

It's Okay to Pause

The quote, "The way you do one thing is the way you do everything," is often attributed to Ralph Waldo Emerson, an American essayist, poet, and philosopher who lived in the nineteenth century. It serves as a reminder to take into account areas that may need to improve in your life.

I noticed the habits and behaviors I exhibited by speaking and rushing through to get my words out, carried over into other areas of my life. In other words, how I was trying to force my words out was also how I was trying to force results to show up in my life. I was desperate to get out of the rut I was in. I was scrambling to find a job, because I didn't have any income or way to take care of myself. In the same way, I was panicking about not being able to speak. How I approached being unemployed was exactly how I handled the interview. You could hear the angst and uneasiness, even though the words refused to escape my lips.

Sometimes in life, we get so caught up in our own ambitions that we never take time to pause. There is no shame in slowing down to catch our breath. In fact, it is in those moments of stillness that we often find answers we need.

We rush from one thing to the next, always in a hurry, always busy. But in the midst of all that chaos, we miss out on the beauty of life.

As a child, I remember watching cartoons on Saturday mornings. I had to hurry to take a bathroom break, get more cereal, and put up

Y.O.U.

the laundry my mom had told me to do before she left for errands in between commercial breaks because we didn't have a pause button on the TV. It was a rush to get everything done before the show came back on. We're in a rush with time feeling like we don't have enough of it but we actually do. It's about prioritizing what's most important.

Technology has advanced over the years. We have so many different apps and platforms that offer us the luxury of pausing our shows and movies whenever we want. Yet, despite the growing convenience of technology, we are busier than ever before.

It's like the world is constantly advertising to us, telling us to hurry up and move on to the next thing. We're bombarded with messages that make us feel like we're falling behind if we're not constantly doing something productive. We're told that time is money and that we need to make every second count.

But in the midst of all this rush, we forget to slow down and take a breath. We forget to appreciate the simple pleasures of life that make it so sweet. We're so used to rushing around that we don't even know how to slow down anymore. It's like we've forgotten how to take a break. To have fun. To sit in our thoughts. To not be so bombarded with anxiety and stress.

Ecclesiastes 3:1 says, "For everything, there is a season, and a time for every matter under heaven." This verse reminds us that

It's Okay to Pause

there's a time for everything in life, including rest and reflection. We need to remember that life is not a race.

So, the next time you're tempted to rush around and try to get everything done in record time, remember that it's okay to hit that pause button. Take time to appreciate the little things that make it so beautiful.

Emily Dickinson once said, "Forever is composed of nows." Let's make the most of our "nows." Let's not miss the moments that matter, the ones that make life worth living. When we forget to prioritize joy, we lose sight of what's truly important.

Psalm 46:10 says, "Be still and know that I am God." When was the last time you were still? When have you reflected on your relationship with God? When we take the time to be still and listen, we can hear His voice guiding us and leading us in the right direction.

Affirmation

I will get where I'm supposed to be when

I'm supposed to be there.

What is for me will never pass me by.

My future is secure.

Chapter 7

Open Mouths, Open Doors

*"The world is full of opportunities,
but they belong to those who speak up and take action."*
—Unknown

Do you ever catch yourself daydreaming about the life you wish to live? Maybe you long for the freedom to pick up your children from school without being confined to a strict schedule, or the ability to travel the world without any financial limitations. And what about giving back to those who have helped you along the way, or to those who are less fortunate than you? Oh, the joy that would bring!

Think back to the simplicity of childhood, where asking for what you wanted was as natural as breathing. Remember how effortlessly children express their desires, unabashedly seeking what they crave without hesitation or doubt. I recall moments with my own daughter, marveling at how she often received more than she needed simply by vocalizing her desires. It was as if the act of asking opened doors to abundance, revealing opportunities that might otherwise remain hidden.

Now, imagine if we approached life with the same uninhibited boldness as children. What if we dared to articulate our dreams and aspirations with the same fervor and conviction? What if we embraced the idea that simply by asking, we could invite more blessings, opportunities, and fulfillment into our lives?

As adults, we often hold back, fearing rejection or judgment. We hesitate to vocalize our deepest desires, settling for less than we deserve. But what if we dared to break free from these self-imposed limitations? What if we reclaimed the audacity of childhood, allowing ourselves to ask boldly and unapologetically for what we truly desire?

Just imagine the possibilities that would unfold if we approached life with the same openness and curiosity as children.

Your Thoughts Shape Your Reality

Let me tell you, sis, the journey to manifesting these dreams starts with one powerful force—belief. Believe that you are worthy of the life you desire, that you have what it takes to make it happen. Speak it into existence, call it forth with your words, for words have the power to shape our realities.

Open Mouths, Open Doors

You must also see yourself as the person who is capable of achieving your dreams. Visualize yourself living the life you desire, feel the emotions that come with it, and let that vision propel you forward. Remember, you are not a mere spectator in your life but an active participant in the creation of your destiny.

Do not be afraid to open your mouth and ask for what you want. When we speak up, we open doors that we never even knew existed. This is not just a mantra, but a truth that is deeply rooted in faith. Psalm 49:3, "My mouth will speak words of wisdom; the meditation of my heart will give you understanding."

> *I knew that speaking life to myself was the only way I was going to accomplish everything I wanted in life.*

I remember when I was struggling with my speech, "Open mouths, open doors" became my battle cry. I repeated it to myself over and over again until it became imprinted on my soul. It drowned out all the fear and self-doubt that I had behind speaking. I knew that speaking life to myself was the only way I was going to accomplish everything I wanted.

Transform Your Inner Dialogue

Speak life to yourself and believe that you are capable of achieving everything you want in life. Your dreams are not just a figment of your imagination, they are a reality waiting to be manifested—when you open your mouth, you will see the doors begin to open.

It's not always easy to do better once we know better. Breaking bad habits is like trying to climb a mountain. It takes time, intentionality, and consistent effort to make lasting changes. We can't expect to see results overnight.

For instance, I always challenge myself not to drink alcohol for thirty days at the beginning of the year. But if I put myself in environments that tempt me to break that promise, I am setting myself up for failure. We do this to ourselves all the time, and it's to our detriment.

Negative self-talk is like a habit that traps our thoughts and eventually drowns out our dreams. We need to intentionally feed our souls with positive affirmations and create new habits that replace those negative thoughts. Can you honestly tell me something positive that you tell yourself every day? If not, it's time to start speaking life into yourself.

If you want to conquer negative self-talk and self-doubt, you must be intentional about what you feed your mind, body, and soul. Negative self-talk can take many forms, from thoughts that undermine your abilities, like "You're not smart enough," to those that encourage procrastination, like "You can do it later."

Any thought that plants the seed of doubt and inaction in your mind is negative self-talk. And we know that procrastination is the

Examine Your Environment

Your environment plays a crucial role in shaping your mindset, and if you surround yourself with negativity—negative music, entertainment gossip, or constantly surround yourself with people who do not motivate you in a positive way, you will continue to live a defeated life.

Your enviorment seeps into your thoughts and actions. And what's in you, will eventually come out. If you consistently immerse yourself in pessimism and perpetuate constant complaints, you'll contribute to creating a toxic environment.

You need to have the type of conversations with yourself and others that will help you grow, flourish, and achieve your dreams.

> *You need to be your own cheerleader, your own coach, your own motivator.*

Be intentional about what enviornment you're exposing yourself to, because it will eventually manifest into your reality. You need to be your own cheerleader, your own coach, your own motivator. Speak life into yourself, declare affirmations, remind yourself of your greatness, and don't let anyone else dim your light.

It's easy to fall into the trap of living a life that is not really yours. Listening to the opinions and expectations of others can be suffocating, and you end up living someone else's life instead of your own. But the good news is, you can always take your power back. In fact, your future dreams depend on it.

The Power of Self-Realization

I remember the excitement I felt when I landed my first job as an accountant at an oil and gas company right out of college. I was so eager to prove myself and climb the corporate ladder. However, after working there for two years, it was time for my annual review, and things didn't go as expected.

The CFO who hired me had left, and I had a new boss, a woman. As a fellow woman, I thought she would understand and appreciate the hard work I had put in and give me the raise I deserved, especially since the company had a great year and I had worked overtime to meet their demands. But instead, she only gave me a 2% raise and told me it was my fault for taking the initial offer.

Her words stung, and I realized I needed to take back my power and ask for what I deserved going forward. And so I did. I decided to leave my corporate job in the oil and gas industry in 2018, despite making close to six figures and having worked in that industry for over ten years.

At the time, I was a single mom raising my daughter, Aliyah, who was eight, and my little sister, Serenity, who was eleven. It

Open Mouths, Open Doors

wasn't easy juggling work and motherhood, especially when it came to managing time off for my sick days and activities like sports. Corporate America only offered two weeks of vacation starting out, and I had to use those days for everything, leaving me with little to no time off for myself.

Leaving that job was a tough decision, but it was the right one. It allowed me to take control of my life and prioritize my family while pursuing my passions.

Taking a leap of faith and opening up a franchise with my sister would require me to step out of my comfort zone and take a huge risk. But I also knew that if I didn't take that risk, I would never know what could have been.

My sister and I have always been close, even though we are three years apart. As the older sibling, I would always ask her what her dreams and aspirations were. And every time, her response was the same, "Ummm, I'm not sure yet, sister, but I know I hate driving in traffic every day!"

We both shared a desire for something more, something greater than the mundane routine of a nine to five job. And that's when it hit me, why not start a business together? We both had different skill sets and strengths that complemented each other perfectly, and we shared the same passion for creating a life that we truly loved.

Y.O.U.

I had to trust in myself and in God's plan for my life. And so, we took the leap and opened up our own franchise. I remember that lunch like it was yesterday.

> **I had to trust in myself and in God's plan for my life.**

The clinking of glasses and silverware echoed throughout the restaurant. My sister dropped the bombshell that would change our lives forever: "Let's open a Smoothie King franchise!"

I nearly choked on my lemonade, but her excitement was contagious. I could feel the energy coursing through her veins as she talked about the endless possibilities of owning a business. And at that moment, I knew that we were meant to do this together.

As I sipped my drink and processed her words, I couldn't help but think about the smoothies I had enjoyed at Smoothie King over the years, especially the Strawberry Kiwi Breeze.

It wasn't just the idea of owning a Smoothie King franchise that excited us. It was the prospect of creating a business that would impact the health and wellness of our community. And we knew that we had the perseverance and resilience to make it happen. But let's be real, starting a business is no walk in the park. It takes grit, determination, and a whole lot of prayer. I knew that we were going to face obstacles, roadblocks, and setbacks. But we also knew that failure wasn't an option. When you have the power of God on your side, anything is possible.

Building Meaningful Connections

We took the plunge. We dove headfirst into the world of entrepreneurship, armed with a passion for health and wellness and a desire to make a difference in our community. I had already launched "Amoorefitbody," a business in the wellness industry, so I knew a thing or two about what it took to make a business successful. But this was a whole new level of challenge.

Nevertheless, we persevered. We reached out to our network, did our research, and poured our hearts and souls into this new venture. Watching our Smoothie King franchise come to life was nothing short of miraculous.

So if you're sitting there, reading this and dreaming of starting your own business, let me tell you something: you can do it. With a little bit of faith and a whole lot of hustle, you can achieve anything you set your mind to.

As Proverbs 15:22 reminds us, "Without counsel, plans go awry, but in the multitude of counselors they are established." We knew that seeking guidance from someone who had already walked this path would be crucial to our success.

And as we put our faith into action, we began to see the pieces fall into place. God truly does align everything when we trust in Him and take action toward our goals. As James 2:17 reminds us, "Faith by itself, if it does not have works, is dead."

Y.O.U.

Sometimes it's the small, seemingly insignificant moments that can change the trajectory of our lives. For me, that moment came when I was mindlessly scrolling through Facebook and stumbled upon a picture of a woman who had just opened up a Smoothie King franchise. I didn't know her, but something inside me told me that I needed to meet her.

> *Sometimes it's the small, seemingly insignificant moments that can change the trajectory of our lives.*

Without hesitation, I reached out to a mutual friend and asked him who this woman was. Within twenty-four hours, he introduced us in a three-way message, and I had scheduled lunch with her. Little did I know, this lunch would mark the beginning of a life-changing mentorship that would guide my sister and I through the ups and downs of opening our own franchise. That connection taught me the power of our networks.

Our connections, whether through friends, family, or social media, can open doors that we never even knew existed. But it's not enough to simply have a network—we must also have the confidence to speak up and ask for what we want.

As Proverbs 27:17 says, "As iron sharpens iron, so one person sharpens another." This is the beauty of mentorship and networking. When we surround ourselves with people who have been through similar experiences and can offer guidance and support, we become better equipped to face the challenges that come our way.

Open Mouths, Open Doors

But it's not enough to simply collect business cards and attend events. I want to remind you, just as I often remind myself, we must have the confidence to open our mouths and ask for what we want. If we don't put in the work, we won't see results.

Scheduling that lunch meeting changed everything. I could have easily scrolled past that picture, too afraid to ask for help or too unsure of myself to make the connection. But I chose to open my mouth, and that decision opened up a world of possibilities.

When we speak, we have the potential to bring value and blessings into our lives and the lives of others. But it's not just about speaking for the sake of speaking. It's about having the confidence to use our voices intentionally, to ask for what we need, and to share our gifts and talents with the world. And you know what's even more incredible? I've not only been able to build a successful business, but I've also been able to be a better mother and provide a brighter future for my daughter.

That one connection led to a ripple effect of blessings. I'm grateful for the confidence to speak up and ask for what I need. It's truly changed my life and the lives of those around me.

If you're unsure of what you need to do, remember that your network truly equals your net worth. Don't be afraid to open your mouth and speak up. You never know what opportunities or blessings may come your way when you do.

Affirmation

I am committed to the process. I understand that it's in the process where I grow and become the person I've always dreamed of.

Chapter 8

Unveiling the Desires of Your Heart

"Delight in the Lord and He will give you the desires of your heart."

—Psalm 37:4

Imagine living a life where your deepest desires are fulfilled, where you find joy and fulfillment in every area of your life–that's the life that awaits you. Let me tell you a secret: the life you've been yearning for is much closer than you think.

When I was young, my dreams revolved around becoming a wealthy aunt, or what I like to call the "Rich Auntie," spoiling my future nieces and nephews with lavish gifts. Miraculously, those desires were fulfilled. However, what God had in store for me went beyond my imagination. I hadn't anticipated having a family of my own because I was focused on traveling and experiencing the world. Yet, God's plan included my daughter, who became my saving grace. As my journey unfolded, I unexpectedly found myself transitioning into the role of a serial entrepreneur, a path that wasn't initially part of my plan.

Sis, let's talk about Psalm 37:4 for a minute. You know it, girl, "Delight yourself in the Lord, and he will give you the desires of your heart."

> When we truly delight in the Lord, we experience His presence, joy, and peace.

Let me break it down for you. The psalmist is telling us that when we find joy and satisfaction in our relationship with God, everything else in our lives starts falling into place. Our desires become aligned with His will, and He blesses us beyond measure.

It's not about just asking God for anything and everything we want —especially things that don't align with Scripture. *Nope*! It's about seeking His will and purpose for our lives and allowing Him to shape our desires according to His word.

When we delight in the Lord, we position ourselves to receive the abundant blessings that He has in store for us. And, as we trust in Him and follow His guidance, He leads us toward the life that He has designed specifically for us.

Unveiling the Desires of Your Heart

Sometimes we can get caught up in wanting things that are not in line with God's plan for our lives. We may desire things that are not good for us, or that will lead us away from our purpose. But when we delight in the Lord, we allow Him to transform our hearts and renew our minds. Our desires begin to shift from what we want to what He wants for us.

When we truly delight in the Lord, we experience His presence, joy, and peace. It's interesting how people often quote the latter part of Psalm 37:4, but they dismiss the first part of the scripture, which says to delight in the Lord.

The truth is, if we're not operating in the principles within the Word, which is what the Lord delights in, then the desires of our hearts won't be as easily achieved because we're not aligned with the principles of faith.

So what does it mean to delight in the Lord? It means to find joy, satisfaction, and contentment in Him. It means to seek His presence, to meditate on His Word day and night, and to walk in obedience to His commands.

When we delight in the Lord, we position ourselves to receive the desires of our hearts, not because we've earned them or deserve them, but because our hearts are aligned with His will. We'll desire to serve others, to love unconditionally, to walk in humility, and to bring glory to His name.

Y.O.U.

Speak Your Desires Into Existence

In the book of Proverbs 18:21, it is written, "Death and life are in the power of the tongue, and those who love it will eat its fruits." Our words hold tremendous power. They can either bring about life and blessing or death and destruction. Therefore, speaking positively, aligning our words with our desires, and speaking life into existence.

Moreover, in Genesis 1:3, we witness the ultimate example of manifestation: "And God said, 'Let there be light,' and there was light." This verse illustrates the creative power of God's spoken word. Through His divine utterance, the world came into existence. It serves as a foundational example of how spoken words have the power to manifest reality.

> *You are worthy, you are deserving, and you can have the life you desire.*

As bearers of God's image, we possess a similar capacity to speak our world into existence. By aligning our words with our desires and speaking them with faith and conviction, we tap into the creative force that flows through us. We become co-creators with God, shaping our reality according to His will and our deepest desires.

Words are not just a means of communication, they have the power to shape our reality. As a business woman, bestselling author of *Woman Evolve*, and media personality Sarah Jakes Roberts says, "Your words have the power to create or destroy, to bless or curse, to heal or hurt."

Unveiling the Desires of Your Heart

I am humbled by the times I have spoken things into existence. It's as if God is listening, waiting for us to declare our intentions so He can respond accordingly. Do you know how you can bring it even closer? By simply opening your mouth and speaking it into existence.

I know, it sounds too simple, too easy. But trust me, it's true. The power of our words is truly remarkable. So, if you start speaking about the life you desire to live—as long as it aligns with God's word—you're taking the first step towards making it a reality.

It's not just about manifesting our desires. Our words can also be used to uplift and encourage others. We have the power to speak life into their situations and help them see the light at the end of the tunnel.

I want to challenge you today to be intentional about the words you speak. Speak words of love, peace, and prosperity over your life and the lives of those around you. Choose to speak life into every situation.

Now, I can hear you asking, "But Alexis, what if I don't deserve to have the desires of my heart? What if I'm not worthy?" Sis, let me tell you that those thoughts are nothing but lies from the enemy. You are worthy, you are deserving, and you can have the life you desire.

Allow those words to sink deep into your heart and soul. Visualize yourself living the life you desire, feel the joy and fulfillment it brings you.

Y.O.U.

Don't Self-Sabotage Your Success

Self-sabotage can take on many forms. Just as I used to avoid speaking because I didn't want people to perceive me in a certain way, I also avoided doing things I needed to do when I was in a place of sadness and hurt. I procrastinated and evaded certain tasks because of how I saw myself. Perfectionism is another example of how I inhibit progress and prevent taking necessary risks—one of those risks happened to be writing this book! I was on the brink of sabotaging it several times, but I had to keep reminding myself that I had to finish what I started. What happens when you sabotage your own efforts? We can speak life into our dreams and watch them come to fruition, but we can also speak death into them and not act on what we say we want. It all depends on the words we choose to speak and the actions that follow.

Our words are not just mere utterances that disappear into thin air. They carry weight and have the ability to shape our reality. We create an atmosphere of hope and belief that anything is possible. However, if we create an atmosphere of disbelief that things will never work out, they won't. And before we know it, our words have become a self-fulfilling prophecy.

Let's be real, it's easy to self-sabotage our own efforts and limit our potential for success. If you're trying to start your own business, you may question your ability to succeed. If you constantly speak negatively about your skills and capabilities, you may subconsciously

Unveiling the Desires of Your Heart

sabotage your own efforts. You may even start to believe that you are not capable of success and, therefore, not put in the necessary work to make your business successful.

So, how can we stop sabotaging ourselves? Cultivate mindfulness to observe your feelings and behaviors without judgment. By becoming more aware of your emotional responses, you can intervene before self-sabotage occurs. Instead of speaking negatively about ourselves, we can choose to use positive affirmations. We can focus on our capabilities, and speak about them in a positive light.

An example of self-sabotage and speaking things into existence:

Sabotage: "I don't have enough money to start a business, and I'll never be able to secure a loan. It's impossible for me."

Speaking into existence: "Money may be a challenge, but I am resourceful and will find creative ways to fund my business. I declare that I will manifest the resources I need and create a successful business."

Sabotage: "I don't have enough experience or knowledge to start a business, and I'm not sure where to begin. It's too overwhelming."

Speaking into existence: "I may not have all the answers right now, but I am willing to learn and grow. I declare that I will gain the knowledge and experience I need to start and run a successful business."

Y.O.U.

Strengthen Your Desires

A strong desire is something that can drive you to achieve greatness. It's that inner voice that tells you that you are meant for something bigger, something greater than yourself. It's the voice that pushes you to pursue your dreams, even when others doubt you or try to hold you back.

> *You have to be willing to pursue that desire with everything you have.*

When you have a strong desire, it's like a fire that burns within you. It fuels your passion, your creativity, and your drive to succeed. It's that spark that ignites your soul and drives you to keep going, no matter what. But here's the thing—that desire alone is not enough.

Your desires give you the strength and motivation to keep going, to keep striving for your goals and dreams. It's what separates the successful from the mediocre, the ones who achieve greatness, from those who settle for less.

Before you know it, that desire becomes so strong that you can't ignore it anymore. Your mind becomes fixated on it, like when you used to obsess over every member of your favorite R&B group, envisioning yourself as part of the group and rehearsing acceptance speeches for imaginary awards ceremonies! Okay, I didn't pretend to rehearse any speeches, but you know what I mean! But this desire is different—it's deeper, more meaningful.

Unveiling the Desires of Your Heart

It's the longing that you must have when it comes to achieving your dreams.

You have to be willing to pursue that desire with everything you have. Because when you have that kind of desire, there's nothing that can stop you. You become unstoppable, unbreakable, and unbeatable. You become a force to be reckoned with, and nothing can stand in your way.

Sis, I want to encourage you today to focus on that strong desire burning inside of you. Don't ignore it, don't push it aside, and don't give up on it.

We tend to hold those around us to a higher standard than we hold ourselves, especially when it comes to their dreams and goals. We become their accountability partner without even being asked.

I mean, seriously. When was the last time you held yourself to the same level of accountability that you hold others? When was the last time you took a step back from everyone else's goals and dreams and asked yourself, *"What do I want?"* It's easy to get so caught up in helping others achieve their dreams that we forget about our own.

Why do we do this? Why do we put everyone else's dreams ahead of our own? We often prioritize others' dreams over our own for various reasons. It could stem from fear of failure or rejection, feeling obligated to meet others' expectations, or simply lacking clarity and direction about our own aspirations. Additionally, societal norms

Y.O.U.

and pressures may influence us to prioritize external validation or conform to expectations rather than pursue our authentic desires. Whatever the reason may be, stop doing it! We have to start holding ourselves to the same standards that we hold others to when it comes to having our desires.

I know it's hard to put ourselves first sometimes, especially when we're used to putting others first. But trust me when I say this, sis, you're worth it. Your dreams are worth it. And you owe it to yourself to go after them with everything you've got.

So, let's make a pact, shall we? Let's make a promise to ourselves to hold ourselves to the same level of accountability that we hold others to. Let's make a promise to take our dreams just as seriously as we take everyone else's. And let's make a promise to never forget that we are just as deserving of success as anyone else.

We should expect greatness and gratitude from ourselves. We should meditate on these expectations day and night until they become a part of our being. When we hold ourselves to a high standard, we give ourselves permission to live the life we've always dreamed of.

I know this to be true because I did it myself. In 2018, I left my job and became a full-time entrepreneur. The joy and gratefulness I felt was overwhelming. I knew that I wanted nothing more than to help educate others on the mindset it takes to become free and successful.

Unveiling the Desires of Your Heart

I encourage you to ask yourself: What do I expect of myself? Meditate on your answer until it becomes a part of you. And then, go out there and achieve greatness. Because when you expect the best from yourself, you become unstoppable.

> *You can't move forward if you're still holding onto emotional baggage from the past.*

Unveiling the truth of who we are and what we're capable of is a powerful journey. For me, it started when I finally asked myself the hard questions. And once I had that clarity, it was no longer about how I got where I was, but how I was going to get out and never come back.

I know what it's like to be on food stamps and feel like your dreams are out of reach. But I also know that the only person who can truly change your circumstances is you. No one else is going to swoop in and save the day. It's up to you to take control of your life and make the necessary changes.

You can't move forward if you're still holding onto emotional baggage from the past. Embrace a new identity and step into the life you were meant to live.

Reinvention Begins with Forgiveness

Reinvention is the process of consciously transforming oneself, breaking away from old patterns, and embracing new directions in life. The key to reinvention is forgiveness. Forgiving yourself for your past mistakes is a moment of unveiling, of letting go of the old and embracing the new.

Look at yourself in the mirror and repeat these words until you believe it: "Today, I release myself from the chains of past mistakes. I forgive myself, knowing that I am worthy of love, growth, and transformation. With each step forward, I embrace the power of forgiveness to guide me on my journey of reinvention."

As a woman with a Christian background, I know all too well the guilt and shame that can come from straying from the path of righteousness. But I also know that forgiveness is the key to freedom.

We all make mistakes. We're human, it's what we do. But that doesn't mean we have to carry the weight of those mistakes with us forever. Walking through the maze of self-forgiveness demands confronting the shadows of guilt and remorse.

A true testament of this came when my daughter's father and I parted ways, leaving behind a trail of broken dreams. In the aftermath, God's unseen hand orchestrated healing and redemption. It was through the arduous process of forgiving myself and releasing the burden of guilt that I began to untangle the knots of disappointment.

You are still a child of God, and He loves you no matter what. He forgives you every time you ask for it. So why do we make it difficult to forgive ourselves? I believe one of the reasons is because the enemy wants to keep us from having our desires and living in

Unveiling the Desires of Your Heart

freedom. Forgiveness becomes not only an act of self-compassion but also a defiance against the forces that seek to imprison us.

Choosing the path of your passion may be one of the toughest decisions you'll ever make, but it's also the most beautiful.

> *When we are honest with ourselves and others, it fosters trust and respect.*

Your life is the most valuable thing you will ever possess. It's a gift from God that you should cherish and invest in. I know firsthand how it feels to be a new mom, to wonder if you're doing enough for your child. Investing in your personal growth is one of the greatest gifts you can give to your child.

Having my daughter was a turning point in my life. It pushed me to be the best version of myself. It made me realize that I was capable of so much more than I ever thought possible. It's amazing how much strength you can find within yourself when you have someone counting on you to protect and provide for them.

It's not just about being a parent. It's about recognizing your own voice, knowing who you are and the greatness you're capable of achieving. God is counting on you to fulfill your purpose. The gifts He has given you are meant to be shared with the world.

Water that seed and grow in the areas that are most rewarding and fulfilling to you. And if you really want to uncover more talents, ask God and listen for that whisper in your ear. He will tell you, as it says in James 1:5, "If any of you lacks wisdom, you should ask

God, who gives generously to all without finding fault, and it will be given to you."

As Maya Angelou famously said, "The truth is liberating." It means being truthful and straightforward even when the truth may be uncomfortable or difficult to hear. When we embrace the truth, it can lead to positive change and growth. It allows us to recognize areas in our lives where we may need to improve, and it opens the door to healing and self-discovery.

For most of my life, I lived by the rule of treating others the way I wanted to be treated. I believed that if I couldn't say something nice, I shouldn't say anything at all. But as I've grown older and wiser, I've come to realize that sometimes the truth is the only way forward.

We live in a world where honesty and accountability are often hard to come by. Everyone wants to tiptoe around not taking responsiblity for their lives. But if you want to live your best life, you have to be willing to face the truth, even when it's uncomfortable. That means being honest with yourself, holding yourself accountable for your actions, and sharing your feelings while relying on the truth, even when others may not find it easy to accept.

By embracing the truth, we can also develop stronger and more meaningful relationships with others. When we are honest with ourselves and others, it fosters trust and respect. It allows us to communicate effectively and openly, leading to deeper connections.

Heaven and Earth

One of the strategies I personally use to align my goals with God's promises is called Heaven and Earth. It's a simple yet powerful exercise that involves getting a sheet of paper and drawing two lines straight down the middle, creating three columns.

On the left column, I write down my goals and desires–everything I'm hoping to achieve or obtain. On the right column, I write down what's been hindering me from reaching those goals. Finally, in the last, middle column, I write down an action plan to help me bridge the gap between Heaven and Earth.

By identifying the obstacles that stand in the way of my dreams, I can create a plan of action. And as I take steps towards achieving my goals, I have faith that God will meet me where I am and bless my efforts. The promises of God will start to manifest in my life, and I will begin to see Heaven on Earth.

I firmly believe that life is all about discovering how to live in Heaven on Earth. When we realize this, we can live with greater peace and joy, and we can focus on the things that truly matter.

Proverbs 4:7 highlights that wisdom is fundamental, urging us to prioritize understanding above all else. It's crucial to recognize that our worth extends beyond external judgments or societal standards. To achieve a greater understanding of ourselves and others, we can start by practicing empathy and active listening.

By putting ourselves in others' shoes and genuinely listening to their perspectives, we can gain valuable insights into their thoughts and experiences. Additionally, engaging in meaningful self-reflection allows us to explore our own ideologies, leading to a deeper understanding of ourselves and our relationships with others.

While it may be easy to get caught up in the rush of everyday life, it's essential to take the time to be still and listen to God's voice. Through these moments, we can find value in the scenic route and discover the important lessons that God is trying to teach us.

When we stop moving and allow ourselves to go deeper within ourselves, we can understand that heaven is a state of mind. It's a place where we think of nothing else but the presence of God.

Have you ever pondered what it truly means to unveil something? To peel back the layers and reveal what's hidden beneath? "Unveiling" is the act of uncovering, of shedding light on what was once obscured.

Unveiling the heart's desires is like lifting the veil of fog, each revelation bringing clarity to our raw emotions and truths. Understanding ourselves better makes it easier to uncover our heart's

Unveiling the Desires of Your Heart

desires. It's like turning up the brightness on a dimly lit path, making it clearer to see what lies ahead.

If we don't remain in a state of awareness, our true desires can often be overshadowed by external influences and distractions.

It's only when we peel away these layers of interference that we can truly see what our hearts long for and begin unveiling the desires of our hearts.

Affirmation

Every step I take is guided by divine

intervention, leading me toward

my ultimate destiny.

I trust in God's timing and know that

everything will fall into place.

Conclusion

Becoming an author had always been a dream for me. I didn't know what I would write about or how my story could help others, but here I am, putting into practice everything I've shared throughout the pages of this book. Now, it's your turn. My hope is to uncover a path for all to surpass pain, conquer fear, and embrace their potential. The truth is that our greatest pain transforms us, propelling us to seek God *even* more. Through discomfort, we become prepared for God's promises. Growth is the epitome of a successful existence, blossoming from healthy roots, solid values, and healing from our insecurities and fears. When we possess this foundation, we experience true growth—a growth that goes beyond simply existing and continually expands its influence and impact.

This growth involves producing fruit, which has its own beauty and strength. What makes a fruit special? Its eternal nature. As its seeds sprout and grow, a fruit becomes everlasting. Fruits have a lasting effect.

As we reach the end of this book, consider the profound chance to plant seeds wherever you tread, through acts of kindness and words of goodness. Just as changing the root of a plant alters its fruit, our actions can lead to far-reaching effects. However, discovering the root requires digging deep and removing anything that hinders growth.

> *The key to eternal perpetuation lies in the strength of our foundation, supported by deep-rooted values.*

The fruits of our deeds may not always be immediately evident. Sometimes, we're fortunate enough to catch a glimpse of the impact we've had—not to boost our egos, but to remind us of the incredible power we possess to illuminate our surroundings for eternity. The key to eternal perpetuation lies in the strength of our foundation, supported by deep-rooted values. It all comes full circle: The deeper our roots, the greater the fruits we bear. Our roots sustain us, provide us with nourishment, and anchor us to a profound sense of belonging. They give us the strength and stability to weather the storms of life and reach new heights. Just as a tree relies on its roots to draw nutrients from the soil, we rely on our roots to draw strength from our origins and forge ahead with unwavering purpose.

As we reach the closing chapters of this extraordinary journey, let me share with you a profound revelation that has touched the

Conclusion

depths of my soul: It's all about the healing. Stepping out of our comfort zones, facing the pain head-on, and emerging on the other side transformed.

Just pause for a moment and let this sink in. Every act of kindness, every ounce of goodness we pour into someone's life, has the power to change us in ways we can't even imagine. It's like a ripple effect, spreading far beyond what our eyes can see. Like that tree with its delicious fruits—when the sun's warm rays touch it, those fruits multiply, creating more seeds, ready to grow in a whole new cycle of abundance.

And that's exactly how it works in our lives, my friend. Our own acts of compassion and generosity sow seeds of everlasting significance. It's like a never-ending cycle of growth and abundance. Let my story be a guiding light for those who feel lost. So, my friend, as you turn the final page and venture into the next chapter of your life, do it with courage and conviction. Embrace the power within you, for you are a beacon of hope, a catalyst for change. And as you continue your journey, may your love and transformation touch lives far and wide, forever altering the course of our shared human experience.

This is *your* story. It's beautiful, messy, and extraordinary. Embrace it all, find solace in the healing process, and rise above the challenges that come your way.

As I conclude this book, I want you to know that you hold within you a spirit of love, grace, and strength. Let it guide you as you leave

Y.O.U.

your mark on the world. Your faith will create a legacy that will motivate future generations. Your boldness and belief in something greater than yourself will leave a lasting impact, serving as a source of inspiration for those who come after you.

You have the power to inspire those around you. Be your own inspiration. Remember, you didn't come this far just to come this far. This isn't the end—it's just the beginning of Y.O.U.—your own *Yearning of Understanding*. Discover who you are, your desires, and continue to bless others with your presence, receiving the abundant blessings God has in store for you.